I0141686

Abby Still Has Issues

More humor essays and unsolicited opinions from
www.AbbyHasIssues.com

Abby Heugel

Abby *Still* Has Issues

Cover design by Amy Vansant of kidfreeliving.com, but that is a young version of Abby

Abby *Still* Has Issues

DEDICATION

I dedicated my first book, *Abby Has Issues*, to my mom, so I don't feel like I can dedicate this one to her, too. She would get a bit of an ego and start expecting me to pour her beer into a wine glass to look fancy.

The cat? Not so much. I have to get her high on catnip so she will leave me alone long enough to try and write something — more proof that I would be an awesome parent.

So this book is dedicated to anyone and everyone who has ever read anything I've written — even the bad stuff — because all sarcasm aside, you're the ones who keep me relatively sane. I say "relatively sane" because some of you drive me nuts, but without you, I wouldn't have as much material to use for my blog.

So thank you and this is for you — except the person who beeps their horn .03 seconds after the light changes green. For you, I promise I'll shut off my car, lie on the hood and feed birds for an hour.

Enjoy!

CONTENTS

PART 3 (Going) Places

PART 4 Things

FORWARD

Welcome back!

I say, "welcome back" because I'm going to assume that I either roped you into buying my first book a couple of years ago or you found it propping open the door of a portable toilet at a campground somewhere in the rural Midwest, read it and decided to give this one a go in the comfort of indoor plumbing.

Regardless, thank you for reading this book, the second compilation of neurotic essays from my blog at www.abbyhasissues.com.

("Neurotic," not "erotic," although if that will help sell some copies, I can try and slip in a few pictures of me longingly gazing at a new jar of vegan pesto or something equally lusty. Just let me know.)

You might be wondering, "Why write a second book? Do you think anyone will actually buy it?"

Great questions. The answer is that between my full-time job as an editor of multiple trade publications, writing a blog and giving away my content for free to websites that will feature me and negotiating brunch menus with the small woodland creatures in my yard, I felt like I needed something more to do.

Plus, I worry that the Internet will blow up one day because of all the pictures of cats wearing sweaters and fear my writing would be lost forever.

To your second question, I will say I've had at least 12 people ask me to write another book, and 8 of them weren't even related to me or drunk at the time of request.

Because I'm a people pleaser when that pleasing will validate my many insecurities, I decided to cater to my audience of dozens.

Plus, if we're being honest, I think my writing has improved since the first book. In fact, my work has even been featured on The Huffington Post and a few other websites that I'm not sure I can legally mention.

And finally, anyone who knows me knows I'm really into money and image.

I mean, if I sell even 20 copies of this book, the first thing I will buy is my yearly purchase of $4 mascara and hair color from a box (I can stretch out the "good for 28 washes" dye job for what, six or seven months, tops?)

No, my friends, money isn't why I wrote this book either. I've made more money taking back empty beer bottles after a family reunion than I've made from publishing books.

I did it because writing is the one thing I really take pride in, the thing that keeps me afloat when I feel like I can barely keep my head above water. If I can share a little humor with even a dozen people that I am or am not related to that are either sober or half in the bag, then it's been worth it to me.

And I hope it's worth it to you.

But if you hate this book, then I suggest you drink *while* reading it or use it to prop open the door of a portable toilet at a campground somewhere for someone to find.

I'm all about paying it forward.

Sincerely,

Abby Heugel

Headlines from My House

There's nothing like an eye-catching headline to draw you into reading a news story, right? That's why I'm providing you with some Headlines from my House.

However, no stories are attached, only because I don't want to incite jealousy as to how absolutely exciting my life as a swinging single gal really is.

Plot to Kill Spider with Foot Foiled by Thought of Spider Guts on Foot

Brilliant Editorial Composed in Shower Vanishes Upon Turning Off Water

Glasses Thought to be Lost Found Safely on Owner's Head

Poll Reveals Advice from Ozzy Osbourne More Reliable than from Dr. Oz

Citizen's Arrest Nabs Perp Using "flusterated" in a Sentence

Brain of Woman Wearing OveGlove Divorces Her After She Grabs Pan with Hand Not Wearing OveGlove… Again

Creature Under Birdfeeder Thought to be Rabid Badger Revealed to be Overfed Rabbit

Campaign to Launch Acronym for 'So Happy It's Thursday' Losing Momentum

Mensa Letter 'Lost in Mail' After Woman Finds Keys in Freezer

Study Confirms 12 Years of Life Spent Looking for Matching Tupperware Lids

Final Jeopardy Question Answered Correctly; No Witnesses

Fashion Police Arrest Woman Found on Couch, in Pajamas, Eating Garlic Hummus on Friday Night

Decapitated Cat Toy Found Behind Couch; No Plans to Remove Body

Stepdad Contracts Flu. Mom Requests 6-pack to Help Deal with Stepdad Afflicted with "Man Flu"

Owner in Contract Discussions with Dustbuster in Effort to Improve Performance

Michigan Woman, 31, Cites 'I have to shovel again' as Reason for Insanity. Judge Accepts Plea

Bird Found Eating Worm in the Afternoon; Myth Busted

Wanted: Body Double to Stand in at Work; Must Resemble 12-year-old-boy and Excel at Feigning Enthusiasm and Productivity

Rug Burn on Elbows Healing Nicely Week After Diving Behind Couch Upon Hearing Doorbell

Missed Connections: You had snacks

After Unsuccessful Attempts at "Tear here," Bag of Steamable Vegetables Slated to be Opened with Teeth

Planned Productivity Delayed Due to 'Joan and Melissa' Marathon

Rare Triple Axel Performed After Tripping Over Cat; Cat Not Impressed

SWF Seeks Anything to Love as Much as She Loves Pesto

After Witnessing Large Number of Adults Failing to Follow Directions, Kids Given More Credit

Squirrels Picket Outside House; Demand Variety in Local Seed Offerings

Shopper Leaves Target Having Spent Less than $20; Parade Thrown in Her Honor

Writer Attempts Humor with Blog Post; Pulitzer Prize Safe for Now

A Hole in One

Scene 1: I'm walking across the tiled kitchen floor when I feel a cold spot somewhere on the bottom of my sock. I lift up my foot to make sure I didn't step in something and notice a hole there instead.

Scene 2: I'm two minutes into a walk when my underwear either suction themselves into a killer wedgie or are too big and sag down instead.

Scene 3: I'm halfway to work in the morning and realize that I'm wearing the world's most uncomfortable bra, which pretty much describes anything that's not a sports bra.

In all three scenarios, the logical conclusion to each scene would show me removing said article of clothing and promptly throwing it away. After all, they are uncomfortable and/or old and falling apart. I am not a homeless person, and I can afford to buy new socks and underwear and throw the old away.

But I also have a short attention span, so something usually distracts me between "remember to take off those socks and throw them away" and actually taking off the socks and throwing them away. My guess is it's usually something shiny or that makes a cool noise…

The bra is another story.

I have around, oh, one "big girl bra" that I can wear without feeling like a corset is wrapped around my chest.* When that bra is in the wash or I need to wear something else, I have one backup that can pull off the job of pretending to be needed for a day.

*I realize I could go get fitted and get something fancy, but seeing as my concave boobs take up as much real estate as the mosquito bite on my arm, I'm really not willing to pay.

With that said, I have a handful of bras and underwear in my drawer that serve no purpose. They are uncomfortable, but yet they're still there and accidentally worn on occasion simply because I forget, and well, they're still there.

They're like those people you can't stand that you haven't seen for a while. You think, "Maybe I was wrong. Maybe they're not that annoying and I can talk to them without wishing for a Xanax salt lick."

But then "bam!" Two minutes in you realize you should have told them you had to go detail the cat's litter box, or in the case of the underwear, you wish you had simply just thrown them away.

So let this be a cautionary tale to you.

If you have holes in your socks, if the elastic on a pair of underwear you bought in a Hanes six-pack is gone or the bra that you have is causing you to stab yourself in the leg with a butter knife, just throw them away.

Save yourself.

Learn from my mistakes.

Don't be a hero.

*This post is brought to you by the uncomfortable bra I accidentally wore to work and the hole that I found in my sock. Again.

I Smell

A majority of the decisions I make on a daily basis are at least partially the result of the "smell test." Maybe it's because I have a big nose, but my first instinct when given something—be it food, a puppy or even a candle specifically labeled "unscented"—is to smell it.

I'm just a "smelly" person.

My bedroom dresser has everything from candles and reed diffusers to lotions and perfumes — various vehicles for delightful scents.

Other rooms in my house have more subtle touches —a Glade Plug-In in the bathroom, a candle in the living room, room spray throughout, etc.

Now before you go making assumptions, let me point out that I don't stink and overcompensate for that fact with these things. I smell just fine, even delightful at times.

But I'm still a "smelly" person.

I've been this way for as long as I can remember. When I was just a little one with issues, I had a white blanket with fringe on the end and I would wrap a clump of the fringe around my little finger before pulling it off and smelling it while I sucked my thumb.

We apparently called this "Nonny Nose," although I don't remember that part and surely would have come up with something more clever had 3-year-old me been given the option.

But here's where it gets interesting, as after the blanket, there was Bun—an unfortunate stuffed bunny.

Instead of bringing the fringe up to my nose when I sucked my thumb, it was his left ear—almost always the left one. Why? Because I slept on my right side—always facing the door in my room—and so his left ear was closest to me.

He slept on his back.

I can't tell you exactly what it was about that first in a series of OCD rituals, but I can tell you I remember thinking that his *(snot and spit-covered ear)* smelled different with my thumb in my mouth. Also, the left ear was superior to the right and if I didn't suck my thumb and smell his ear, I wouldn't be able to sleep.

When we traveled up north to our trailer in the summer, I would sleep on the top bunk of our triple bunk beds. Because I often fell out, we had a bed rail. Because Bun often fell out, we tied a shoestring around his neck noose-like and secured him to said bed rail.

A bit dark, yes, but it did the trick.

Bun went everywhere and did everything and his body showed the wear and tear of being loved a little bit too much. It was a sad day when I finally let go of his scrawny little neck, but my dates were getting uncomfortable with the fact I let him keep his side of the bed.

I'm kidding, of course. But from blankets and Bun to other things that don't start with "b," I'm just a "smelly" person.

I see, I touch, I smell — even delightful at times.

But most certainly better than Bun.

Bleep It Out

I'm told when I was little, one of the first phrases I uttered was "Goddamn dog." This is due largely in part to the fact that my grandma used to throw it around on the regular when their geriatric poodle would jump on the back of the couch.

She still denies that she influenced an impressionable toddler to wander around the house mumbling profanities at a senile poodle, but from what I can recall, there was never an episode on Sesame Street in which Big Bird was bleeped out.

I share this little tidbit because I'm going to continue to talk about cursing. While I figure most of my readers are used to me, there might be one or two that are new and accidentally ended up here by searching "squirrels wearing Polish babushkas."

In that case, this is your warning.

Although I don't remember the dog incidents, I do remember the first time I ever stuck up my middle finger. I think I was around six or seven, and oddly enough, I was by myself and sitting on the toilet in our laundry room. *(Why I remember this detail but spent 10 mins. looking for the keys I left in my back door last week is beyond me.)*

I remember that I heard it was bad to do, but had no idea what it meant. The first time I did it it felt foreign and strange, like eating with a fork in your opposite hand. But I couldn't figure out why one finger meant so much and soon got bored with the idea.

Fast forward about 10-15 years.

While I grew taller, both my boobs and my internal filter failed to mature and develop. A good student, athletic and innocent for the most part, the fact that I had the mouth of a drunken sailor was my dirty little secret until I actually opened up my mouth and let it fly.

I haven't outgrown this shit yet.

This comes as a surprise to a lot of people, especially seeing as I keep things rather family-friendly *(if your friends and family are dysfunctional, which most of mine are.)*

I don't ever curse for the shock value or to try and work up street cred I would inevitably lose the second someone witnessed me walking around with a forgotten Velcro roller in my hair. Sometimes I'll put it in a cuss word because it's part of the situation, but otherwise I don't think profanity really adds to my posts.

But in person, email or texts with "appropriate" parties, it's a different *(often R-rated)* story.

I figure I don't smoke. I very seldom drink. I try to limit my use of voodoo dolls to less than an hour a day. If choosing to express myself in a colorful way is the worst thing that I do, then dammit, so be it. Except I'm pretty sure it's not the worst thing that I do.

Shit.

What I mean is that choosing to express myself in a colorful way *in appropriate situations* doesn't really hurt anyone else, and although I've accidentally let it slip within the confines of questionable company more than once, I'm generally very respectful of my use of salty language.

And to people who say profanity is just something people with low intelligence use as a crutch, I call bullshit. I feel I have a pretty good handle on how to use the English language and I know when to add in the filter, but sometimes nothing but a good ol' "shit on a shingle" will do.

So while I'll continue to watch my language when needed, just know that if you ever hang out with me or send me an email that opens up the door for an inappropriate comment, I'll take that shit and run with it.

I'll blame my grandma—or perhaps that damn dog.

A Letter to My New Yoga Pants

I understand you had higher hopes for where you'd end up, maybe some fashion-forward type with a perky butt that would fill you out better than I can and wear you only once every few weeks while "slumming" and sipping wine on a veranda.

However, the simple fact is that I chose you to come into my life and join a rotation of about three other pair of these pants. You play the hand you're dealt.

I need to make clear up front that even though I will wear you when occasionally doing yoga, I'm aware you're not technically yoga pants—you're workout pants.

I don't pretend that you're a $100 purchase from Lululemon that I'll never buy when you're actually a $12 purchase from Target, but seeing as I don't sip wine and eat sushi on a veranda, please allow me to sound fancy when referencing you.

I also need to make it clear that for me, you aren't just weekend wear or something to lounge in.

You will become a highly valued member of my family. Because you're new, you will be considered my "good yoga pants" and will be worn to the gym, the store, etc.—in other words, you will be a public figure of sorts.

That means I'm going to need to rely on you day in and day out until I feel others get suspicious and I throw you in the wash.

This cycle will continue until you literally wear out your welcome, like the others who have journeyed before you.

When that time comes, be secure in the knowledge I will keep you around as my "home" yoga pants, which is a pretty much like retirement in the Florida Keys for you.

Public appearances will be replaced with home workouts and actual yoga sessions, but your primary function is comfort.

Every day when I get home from work, you are expected to be standing guard at the ready, next to the sports bra and T-shirt that complete my fashionista trifecta.

There will be challenges—cat hair, spilled food, quick sprints outside to try and move the recycle bin out to the curb on the days I remember—but when all is said and done, you will know that it's you and you alone who provide me with a sense of relief and relaxation from "real" pants that just don't get me.

So welcome to the rotation, my friend.

I look forward to breaking you in.

Couchgating 101

Unless you're new here, you know that I love sports. If you're new here, you should know that I love sports.

I watch them on TV. I listen to sports talk radio 95 percent of the time. If someone approaches me for an intelligent discussion about baseball or anything/anyone on ESPN, it's like flipping a switch. You instantly have my attention.

Sports get me. I get sports.

But I have to confess that as much as I love watching and talking about the games, I don't always enjoy watching the games *at* the games. Overpriced parking, $5 bottles of water and expensive tickets just to sit in a cramped seat next to a drunken fool who spends the whole game screaming obscenities through a bullhorn? No thanks.

I know, I know. Nothing can replace the atmosphere of attending an event live and I do enjoy going once in awhile, but with few extreme exceptions, the only thing I'm parking is my ass on the couch.

My couch gets me. I get my couch.

So what do you get when you combine sports and the couch? Couchgating*, the underrated yet superior alternative to traditional tailgating and game viewing.

Unlike the rigid rules associated with attending an event—*parking passes, assigned seats, having to wear pants*—couchgating is much more relaxed, greatly improving the game day experience.

If you want to wear your favorite jersey, paint your face and ring a cowbell—*looking at you mom*—you can do so without judgment or death threats *(depending on your neighbors, of course.)*

And if you're going more casual, you can even wear a cat hair-covered robe and judge every missed call like a much poorer, sports obsessed Judge Judy without anyone giving you "the look."

"The look" can also be seen — *and appropriately given* — when stuck behind people on the concourse walking ridiculously slow who won't let you pass as you try and make your way up to the concession stand.

Once there, said people will scour the limited menu as if deciphering Egyptian hieroglyphics, delaying your ability to secure an overpriced water bottle that will send you to the germ-infested toilet or claustrophobia-inducing Petri dish known as a Porto-Potty multiple times.

At home, there are no concession concessions *(see what I did there?)* needed, and the option to use a working toilet instead of climbing through rows of disgruntled fans to secure a spot in a 20 minute line to evacuate your bladder of the $5 water pretty much seals the deal for me. *(In case you're new here and haven't left yet, I have a bladder the size of a Cheerio.)*

I also overshare.

Anyway, the only "obstructed view seats" at home are when the cat does her rendition of "Riverdance" in front of the TV to get my attention/catnip, the Wave can be done on *your* schedule without the pressure of waiting for *your* turn to stand and if the game sucks, you can just change the channel.

So while I admit that going to games can be fun, at the end of the game day for me, you know where I'll probably be.

Couchgating gets me. I get couchgating.

*Note: In warmer weather, couchgating is replaced with deckgating, which is similar in structure but necessitates a lawn chair on the deck and a radio.

Holy Sheet

We all have certain chores that we don't mind doing. Some people prefer washing dishes over vacuuming or taking out the trash over dusting the shelves. If you have more than one person at home, these tasks can be split up accordingly.

But when you live alone—or with a cat who still hasn't pulled her own weight—all of these tasks fall to you. And aside from ironing, I have to say one thing I find extremely tedious is changing the sheets on my bed.

Let's examine the process.

It starts with simply ripping off the covers and throwing the pillows and blankets in a heap on the floor with dramatic flair—and about 1/100th of the time it will take me to remake the bed.

It's at this point I realize there's no turning back and swallow a small lump of panic. With the old sheets in the basket and the new sheets still folded in a pile, I am now committed to following through with the process if I want to sleep on sheets ever again.

Ever again!

Exhausted by the thought, I take the sheets from the shelf and let them rest on the bed for a bit while I rest for a bit on my own.

I will usually get *(intentionally)* distracted by something more interesting like watching the squirrels and cursing Disney movies for leaving me so disillusioned about small woodland creatures and their willingness to help me with chores.

But I steel myself up and return to my task, plowing through the bottom sheet and two pillows and fighting with the corners of death.

You know what I'm talking about.

The only thing harder than fitting the elastic-ish corners of the bottom sheet across each of the four ends of the mattress without one popping off every time is actually folding the bottom sheet when it comes out of the dryer.

Tedious.

Enter a quick break to test out the sheets and pillows, at which point I stare at the ceiling and decide I should probably wipe off the ceiling fan at that exact minute.

About 20 minutes later I continue on with my journey of placing the top sheet on with equal amounts of sheet on either side of the bed.

But no matter how hard I try, I end up walking back multiple times to pull the sheet a little bit more on one side before tucking it under the mattress.

If it's too short on one side, I end up pulling the whole thing out when I get into bed. If I pull it too far up the front, my feet will poke out of the bottom and there's a good chance I'll wake up with the excess sheet wrapped around my head and panic that the cat's trying to smother me.

Yup, still single, people.

Anyway, once sheet side distribution is complete, I triumphantly throw on the blanket with the flair of a matador waving his flag. After ensuring equal blanket distribution—*see sheet step above*—the task is finally complete a mere 45 minutes or so later.

Holy sheet.

I'm exhausted just thinking about it, but at least now the bed will have sheets.

Lashing Out

I don't mean to brag, but I think I can confidently say that I have perfected the role of a perpetual "Before" picture when it comes to day-to-day beauty.

While I will occasionally splurge and risk life, limb and sanity to get my eyebrows waxed, more often than not my attempts at beauty wind up with me at work with a forgotten Velcro roller in my hair, resentment over having to wear a real "big girl" bra *(for social convention, not out of necessity)* and chicken tracks under my eyes from sneezing while applying mascara.

I just have no interest, and we're past the point of no return.

But I do wear a little foundation and a coat of mascara, which is what brings me to my point today. I had to buy new mascara.

What. The. Hell. People.

I had a $2 coupon for Cover Girl, so I went to the store to find out how to be Easy, Breezy and Beautiful — *which sounds a bit slutty, yet intriguing* — and was bombarded with approximately 405 different options.

I could be a Lash Fanatic or engage in Lashperfection, Lashwrap, Lashblast Fusion, LashExact, Luxe, Mousse and an All-In-One professional option that I assume will also staple and collate any inner-office memos in a passive aggressive way.

I needed a coupon for liquor at that point — not something that promised Eye Brightening with an Elasta-Nylon formula.

So even though I didn't have a coupon for Maybelline, I shifted my minimally mascara-ed gaze over to that section in a quest to answer the eternal question: "Maybe she's born with it? Maybe it's Maybelline?"

More like, "Maybe it's a crap shoot?"

Here I was presented with 4,367 different options that specialized in curl, definition, length, long wearing, volume, washable, waterproof, Volum'Express, XXL curl, Lash Stiletto and Lash Discovery with promises that with a swipe of a *(curved, flexible, stiff or extended)* wand, I could have dramatically curled, extended, mega plush up to 85 or 300 percent visibly longer lashes amped up 3, 5, 7, 9, or 11 times the normal volume.

All without clumps.

THIS IS WHY OTHER COUNTRIES HATE US!

While L'Oreal promised to "millionize" my lashes, that sounded like entirely too many. As it is, my meager eyelashes often end up in my eyes—*way to do your job of keeping crap out of my eyes, eyelashes!*—and having a million around would just complicate things. So even though the packaging was screaming, "Because you're worth it!" I really didn't think it was worth jabbing my fingers in my eyes to retrieve a million voluptuous lashes — or $9.

But that's not all!

It also turns out that when mascara just isn't enough — *I know, how could it not be with all of these options?*— one can also invest in eyelash extensions and prescription eyelash enhancers. In other words, Rogaine and Viagra for eyelashes.

I can only imagine the product development team at these companies had a three martini lunch when this particular idea was tossed out there on the table.

Let's just file it under "things that don't need to be things."

Anyway, after weighing my options I defaulted to the same $5 mascara I've been buying for years—*the basic Maybelline in the pink tube*—answering the question that yes, those chicken tracks under my eyes *are* Maybelline.

Because, after all, I'm worth it.

Take Notes, Hollywood

As I was fishing chickpeas out of the sink the other day, I was reminded that I'm why I can't have nice things—and also why I will never have a movie made about my life.

But if Lifetime's Meredith Baxter-Birney retires from storylines involving a drug-addicted woman scorned by conjoined twin husbands and decides to go a new route—enter my life as a movie—I have a few suggestions for the writers.

- A montage of me wandering around the kitchen wondering why I went in there, each scene featuring a different, stylish T-shirt.
- Plot twists around why the cat's head is wet and covered in catnip and an existential crisis upon realizing the excitement for electric tweezers exhibited by people in infomercials far exceeds any emotional reaction I've ever had for anything with my job.
- Simple dialogue involving key phrases such as, "I'm confused," "Not now, I'm eating," "Ouch" and "Why is there such a high divorce rate among my socks?"
- Marvin Gaye's "Let's Get it On" would play every time I sit down to eat a meal, with "I Am Woman" supplying the background music every time I remember to put out the recycle bin.

And if you need more storylines, it might be helpful to take a look at a few of my tweets from the past couple of weeks.

A squirrel just ran by the deck with a piece of bread. If another one shows up with a Mimosa, does this count as hosting a brunch?

As she watched her little dog pee into the wind, she took pride in the fact at least this time, he didn't tip over.

"That girl graduated from college and still goes out in the snow in PJs and flip-flops to fill the feeder. Money well spent." – My neighbors

If they don't want an impromptu dance party in the store, they shouldn't play Michael Jackson's "Shake Your Body (Down to the Ground.)"

Tortillas are like little warm blankets for food.

"The best option here is to panic." – My brain when I think that I've lost my ChapStick.

Days when my underwear matches my outfit make me feel like I've really got it together.

I came across two decapitated Barbie torsos on the sidewalk. I'm disturbed, yet slightly intrigued.

When I'm feeling down, I make a list of things to look forward to. Today's just said "food" and "sleep." Pretty good list.

"You must do the thing you think you cannot do" she said to herself as she prepared to say Worcestershire sauce.

I dreamed about work last night and now I'm at work. I'm not impressed with this "living the dream" thing.

The irony of watching "Fashion Police" while on the couch in yoga pants isn't lost on me.

Becoming a member of the Swiffer Facebook Fan Club is the closest I'll ever come to joining a gang.

I'm for equal rights so I just used the often neglected back left burner on my stove. Follow my lead, people.

"Be the change that you wish to see in the world," I whisper to myself as I replace the empty paper towel roll in the office kitchen.

My one-woman show "Help Me I'm Trapped In my Sweatshirt!" is garnering some major buzz from the cat.

My Sunday morning walk of shame includes a fabric softener sheet falling out of the leg of my pants at the gym.

Again, that's just a sample. I suppose that means several sequels could be made, not to mention a line of action figures featuring a variety of interchangeable workout pants and sweatshirts tinged with the light scent of garlic.

All I ask is that the bust region resembles more "Barbie" than "Skipper." Let's make this happen, people.

The Negotiator

The other day I came home to a chipmunk domestic in my yard. It was like COPS: Small Woodland Creature edition, minus the mini wife beater tanks and camera crew.

Considering there was plenty of food under the feeder for all to enjoy, it made me wonder what could tick off these little buggers so much that they would scream and chase each other around the yard. Does he always leave the seat up? Does she only cook up corn?

Yes, I spent a few moments pondering this.

Perhaps I've just been watching CSI: NY for too long. It's pretty much the only "serious" show that I'll watch on TV, due in part to the fact I feel a special connection with Gary Sinise after he and his Lt. Dan Band — yes, it's a thing — were the entertainment at a Halloween party about five years ago.

But I do like the characters and the show, despite the fact each episode would only last about 20 minutes if you took away the music and shots of the medical examiner looking fascinated every time he picked up a scalpel *(accompanied by aforementioned music.)*

While I don't live in New York and am fairly confident that I'm not part of an underground Mafia ring, I am a little hyperaware of certain things.

I think people sitting in their cars in empty parking lots look creepy— even if they're just taking a lunch break, going into a bank makes me feel like I'm part of "Oceans 11" minus the hot guys and I assume anyone who pulls up behind me at an ATM is the Unibomber out for a jaunt.

But if *(god forbid)* something did every happen to me, I'm pretty sure I would be the world's worst hostage.

The perps would most likely "remove me from the situation" quickly or surrender to authorities ASAP, preferring jail to my incessant requests to get home in time to watch the new "Chopped."

Along with the wrath of me missing my TV show, they would have to contend with the fact I drink water all the time. Drinking water all the time combined with a bladder the size of a Cheerio means I have to go to the bathroom every five minutes.

And hell hath no fury if this "situation" falls within any of the five windows during the day in which I engage in my feedings.

If for some reason things did get carried away and a ransom note was required, the criminal would have to let me put my artistic OCD skills to use in cutting out all the letters from magazines myself. In addition, I would need to edit and possibly revise said ransom note before it could be sent out to authorities.

If it has my name on it, I want it to look good.

At any rate, the news description of what I was wearing when I went missing would probably cause my family to pretend they don't know who I am. "Yoga pants, a sweatshirt and a streak of hummus in her hair? Nope, I don't know her."

That would be unfortunate because I'm pretty sure the criminal would ante up funds simply to send me away if my above requirements weren't met. After all, I have chipmunks to feed, and apparently you don't want to piss those guys off.

You never know what they can do.

Philosophizing

The other day I was philosophizing and asked, "If a writer posts something that nobody reads, does her head make a sound when it bangs on the desk?"

The resounding consensus was that yes, it does make a sound, and it's often loud enough to scare a cat or small children who are within earshot of said desk. Profanity — or "flowery, colorful language," as I prefer to call it — might also accompany that sound.

But I have to think that anyone who has ever written something more than a grocery list has experienced that "head desk" moment of self-doubt and frustration after sharing their work.

You can have the best idea EVER — better even than the OveGlove — and proudly hit publish before sitting back to bask in the glow of praise from the masses. Links will be shared! Comments will be left! You vow to stay humble and remember your roots!

But it stays dark for a disturbingly long time, even upwards of 10 minutes or so *(we're talking writer time here.)* There's no immediate glow to bask in. In fact, there's not even a spark.

So you go back and read it over again. Still convinced that you hit a home run, you tweet out the link one more time and decide to go start jotting down notes for the next post.

The next post?

Crap. What the heck are you going to write about now? Considering no one liked the last post you put up 15 minutes ago, the pressure's on to come back with something better, something that will really knock them all dead.

Maybe a post about how you don't care what people think or if they ever read the stuff that you write? Or maybe a funny take on the writer's block that everyone gets — everyone does get writer's block, right?— except it wouldn't be that funny considering you're convinced you'll NEVER BE FUNNY AGAIN!

Taking a deep breath, you resist the urge to just start posting things to stay relevant — you don't want to be "that" girl — and instead get the cat high with catnip. The tolerance she seems to have built up only slightly disturbs you, but her requests for rolling papers *do* set you on edge.

To distract yourself, you check for external validation from strangers on the Internet...still nothing.

Emotionally drained at this point, you stare forlornly into your sparsely populated liquor cabinet and think, "I'm an artist, dammit. I can't work under these conditions."

Then you remember that you don't really drink and that your flair for drama has clouded the fact that your sparsely populated liquor cabinet is actually the shelf with your toaster and steamer.

You take that as a sign from the universe to feed your feelings, after which you send yourself an email just to make sure it still works.

It still works. So you sigh. Dramatically. And bang your head on the desk.

The cat rolls her eyes before leaving the room.

So goes the life of a writer.

A Silver Lining

Do you have an extra hour?

If so, I invite you to watch me attempt to put up a new shower curtain liner.

This is a task that must be done on a regular basis, lest one plans on growing an assortment of invasive species in their shower. But it's often complicated by a) the ridiculous metal rings that have to be opened and closed and b) the fact that I'm me.

It starts with the purchase of the $5 vinyl liner from Target, simply because I'm fancy, and then the placement of the packaged liner on the counter for at least two weeks while I muster up the motivation to enter into this bathroom battle.

Once I feel sufficiently motivated and occasionally medicated, I pull out the scissors and cut down the old liner. This saves me the work of opening the ridiculously stubborn hooks for at least a few minutes more.

After the old liner is properly discarded though, the real work begins.

With an air of demented determination, I set out to pinch open the bastard hook things as fast as I can, trying to ward of the agonizingly painful feeling of having to hold up my arms for what feels like at least two or three hours.*

about 10 minutes

Once the rings are all open and I regain the feeling in my separated shoulders and numb arms, I pat myself on the back — *it's good to recognize small victories* — and begin hanging up the new liner.

This is a relatively easy part of the process, what with the rings already open, but it never fails that I step into the shower to hang the thing up and step in one random small droplet of water.

27

If there's not a helpline for people who step in small droplets of water with clean socks on while changing the shower curtain liner, there needs to be.

Or I could just remember to take off my socks.

At any rate, once the new liner is hung and a second congratulatory break is taken, I set out to pinch shut the bastard hook things as fast as I can, trying to ward of the agonizingly painful feeling of having to hold up my arms for what feels like at least two or three hours.*

about two or three minutes

When the last hook is snapped, I can exhale, change my socks and take comfort in the fact that I won't have to do this again for at least a few months.

Unless I did it wrong and missed a hook somewhere along the way, in which case I will cry and have an extra hook hanging around for a bit.

Then again, it's one less hook left to close.

Phoning It In

Don't take it personally, but if you call my phone and expect to talk to me at that exact moment, you'll probably get my voicemail.

This is *(probably)* not because I hate you.

This is because I hate talking on the phone.

I don't really regard this as anti-social behavior — *I have plenty of those that I can easily identify* — because I will text, email and talk face-to-face with no issue, at least for a short amount of time.

And I also understand the importance of talking on the phone in certain circumstances and do so when the situation requires it, but for the most part, I'll do pretty much anything to avoid using it for more than casual check-ins.

I know this can be annoying, but I have my reasons.

Random Ringing

I don't like not knowing when the call is coming in. When forced to engage in spontaneous conversation without warning, I don't have time to think up an appropriate reply. This means I could get caught saying any number of ridiculous things simply because I couldn't prepare what would most likely be an equally ridiculous excuse quick enough.

I do better if I am initiating the phone call myself, as I can prepare for the communication and sometimes even "rehearse" the call by going over possible responses in my head. But random ringing? No bueno.

Thank goodness for caller ID.

Wrap It Up

I have no problem exiting a phone conversation. It's getting others to realize that I want to exit the conversation about five minutes ago that's the problem.

You see, "long story short" is usually anything but. When my exaggerated sighs and verbal hints to wrap things up and get to the point are ignored in favor of minute story details, I am forced to start banging pots and pans or slamming doors to give the illusion of being extrasuperbusy.

But if all else fails, I can always use the "my phone cut out" excuse. Given the fact that my phone is cheap and does cut out often, this probably isn't a lie.

No You Go…No You!

Despite "great" reception, people often end up talking over each other on the phone. Conversations usually end up sounding like they're on some sort of tape delay and consist of both people talking at the same time, and then pausing, and then talking again at the same time, and then pausing…

It's completely disjointed and frustrating, and by that point I will have simply forgotten why I called you in the first place. Then I will remember that you probably called me.

I rarely dial out.

Distracted Dialing

Here's the deal.

People are always doing other things while they're talking on the phone. Unless they're chained to a landline, you can bet they're watching TV, surfing the Interwebs, driving or — lord help me — on the crapper while attempting to carry on a conversation.

If you're going to call me, please focus on that and not if anyone "liked" your witty Facebook status. And if I'm in a bathroom and hear you on your phone telling someone that you're at your desk or the mall, I will continuously flush the toilet for no reason other than to blow your cover.

If you have a problem with this, just have your people call my people — and leave a message at the tone.

My Hairy Little Roommate

Even though I adopted a cat, I'm not a cat person.

Before you freak out, let me add the disclaimer that Monie is an awesome cat and I love her. But I'm a neurotic weirdo who's still trying to be Zen about having this walking hairball that demands affection, sheds and forces me to say, "No lickey!" entirely more than I'm comfortable with.

But we're roommates, and to be honest, I probably have the better part of the arrangement.

While I have to deal with a creature that makes Gremlin noises and leaves the occasional hairball on the carpet—*dramatic sigh*—she has to deal with me jumping around the living room yelling with Jillian Michaels, dancing with the Swiffer and making up songs about catnip while trying to get the cat high.

The last verse of which is usually something about how I'll probably die alone.

Anyway, here are some things I've learned these past few months:

- If there is a Hell, it's covered in cat hair. If there is a Heaven, it includes the Bissell Pet Hair Eraser. And million dollar idea: yoga-type pants that are made of the same stuff as lint brushes. Run with that, people.
- She does not enjoy me making her little arms "raise the roof" to "Hip Hop Hooray," but she does seem to take delight in watching me try and capture a fly for 10 minutes. I think we're doing this wrong.
- Although she's great about giving me my space when I workout, 40 minutes of yoga calm is instantly negated by the sound of her hacking up a hairball in the next room. Namaste.

- I never feel more inferior than when she watches me scoop out her shitbox. It's not that she's mocking me, but I swear her gaze says, "More enthusiasm, and with a smile. You missed a spot."
- While many cats are motivated by food and reinforce the "I want affection for 1.2 seconds, after which time I will claw you to escape from your overbearing presence" stereotype, she does neither. On the other hand, I just described myself.
- The term "scaredy cat" doesn't really apply. I can "Riverdance" across the living room floor or yell at her for making risotto like a fat cow while watching "Kitchen Nightmares" and she doesn't budge. The vacuum does provoke a little fear, but that could be because I usually end up lassoing the ridiculously long cord around like a demented cowgirl.

But unlike stories I've heard about other roommates, I've never come home to find she went on a crazy *(catnip)* bender that resulted in her piercing her multiple teats and ordering mass quantities of Snuggies off QVC. And while she has yet to pay rent or learn how to flush, she can make me laugh and puts up with my neurosis while simultaneously contributing to it.

I just thank god this cat can't blog.

Withdraw Symptoms

I'm pretty sure the Pope and his posse could pull up behind me in the Popemobile at the ATM and I would still think they were plotting to mug me or judge me for taking too long to complete my transaction.

In my defense, I had never even used an ATM until I was 30. I have no idea why that was, but I have since remedied the situation and can say I've probably used one in an excess of two dozens times since that first jaunt. However, like most mundane activities, I can find something to complicate the situation.

A normal person would simply drive up to the machine, insert their card, enter in their PIN, complete their transaction, grab a receipt and move on with their life. In case you are new here, I'm not entirely normal.

While there are moments of ATM glory, there are also moments of shame and most of those moments look something like this:

- Drive up to cash machine
- Reverse back the required amount to align car window to machine
- Set parking brake, put the window down, glance around to make sure no one is lurking nearby
- Grab purse and try to pry the debit card out of my wallet
- Find mint and get distracted by my good fortune
- Focus on card and then swear as it refuses to budge out of my wallet
- Turn the radio down—too distracting
- Precariously hang out of the window to insert card
- Attempt to insert card into machine
- Re-insert card the right way up
- Glance around again for would-be muggers
- Enter PIN
- Enter amount of cash required
- Press cancel and re-enter correct amount of cash required
- Back up the car again to retrieve an envelope for soon-to-be-delivered cash

- Retrieve cash and receipt
- Glance around again for would-be muggers
- Grab purse and place cash and receipt inside
- Look for another mint but find only disappointment
- Drive forward two feet
- Reverse back to cash machine
- Precariously hang out of the window to retrieve card
- Grab wallet again and shove card into the slot provided
- Silently memorize the facial features of the irate male driver/would-be mugger in line behind me
- Drive forward two feet
- Bath my hands in sanitizer
- Move on with my life

You see how exhausting this is?

No wonder I held off so long.

A Dozen Delusions

It's very important to be honest, but we all have those little things we tell ourselves that we know probably aren't completely accurate. I hesitate to call them "lies," as that implies some sort of deliberate manipulation, so perhaps calling them "delusions of grandeur" would be a bit more accurate.

With that said, I have included short list of the things I tell myself without entirely believing.

---

1. I don't need to write something down because I'll remember it. Despite the fact I don't have solid evidence to back this one up, I continue to employ this philosophy. Mental note—real notes work better.

2. Pushing the pedestrian crossing button at crosswalks actually makes the light change quicker. Is it magic that the little white person on the light appears 10-20 seconds after I push it or simply coincidence? I also tell my self I won't actually say "Ped Xing"— as in "ped exing" and not "pedestrian crossing"— out loud, but I do.

3. That I'll be able to put a key on a key ring in less then 10 minutes. I don't believe this is humanly possible without the use of heavy machinery, yet I still wrestle with the damn things each time.

4. When going to Target, I tell myself I only need one or two things and to act in a civilized manner. Yet a few minutes into my jaunt I more closely resemble a skinny Tasmanian devil who forgot to write down what she needs—see point No. 1—and walks out with a bag full of "prizes."

5. That I can discreetly manipulate two grocery carts that are stuck together, after which point I will be rewarded with a perfectly functional cart for my shopping. However, 99.99 percent of the time, I end up going Hulk on the metal pieces of shit, violently ripping them

apart and being left with one that has a wonky wheel that veers into displays.

6. That faking my own death is an overly dramatic reaction to being asked to attend a webinar or fold laundry.

7. When my phone cuts out, I tell myself to wait a few minutes and let the other person call back. However, I get impatient and am the best at playing the "let's keep calling each other at the same time so it goes straight to voicemail" game. Solution? Avoid the phone.

8. That turning up the radio in my Blazer so I can't hear any weird noise that it's making means there's nothing wrong with my Blazer.

9. Because I feed the squirrels and birds in my yard, I would like to believe they respect me as a neurotic Dr. Doolittle of sorts. But with each acorn that lands on my head by the feeder and each bird gang bang performed in the bird bath, this mutual respect is called into question.

10. That if SpongeBob SquarePants–a *freaking sponge*–can find pants that fit, I can find a pair of "real" pants that aren't uncomfortable. Actually, I don't think I believe this myself anymore and should probably remove it from the list. Let's move on—in workout pants.

11. I clean my floors simply to keep things nice and not because I inevitably drop food every day. Also, that I can stand next to the toaster, anticipating toast, and not jump every time the toast is popped up.

12. That the fact people found my blog with "snowman in a thong and sombrero," "elderly squirrel Fight Club" and "mosquito boobs"—*that one stings*— is cancelled out by whoever found it with "Please. Like you've never Febreezed grandma."

Free for All

I'm pretty careful with my money.

While I'm not quite as bad as my grandma who kept large Ziploc bags in the freezer full of ketchup and mustard packets from various fast food establishments that always gave out "free condiments," I do rinse out Ziplocs on occasion and budget my money appropriately.

Some people buy Prada, I buy produce.

And although I like getting a break on things when I can, people today seem obsessed with getting free stuff. I've seen people practically trample each other for a free unknown sample at the grocery store, a pen at an expo or a 3-hour old hot dog shot out of a weenie gun at a hockey game.

They don't know why they want it, but it's free!

While I used to be one who got excited for free things regardless of whether or not I had any use for them, I really couldn't care less at this point. If it's a great deal, of course I'll run over the elderly and small children to get it. But if it's something I can simply buy for myself if I really want it, I figure I don't need more junk.

Which brings me to a couch in my neighbor's driveway with a "free" sign on it.

Now if you're someone who picks up used furniture that has been sitting outside in February for three days in the driveway of a complete stranger, I apologize in advance, but what the hell is wrong with you?

Let's pretend you're not picking it up to donate to a good cause somewhere because that makes me sound like a witch, and instead work under the assumption that you want a couch for the rec room and thought this would work out.

After all, it is winter and garage sales are scarce. Plus, it's free!

Yes, it is free, and it's probably harboring the bodily fluids of various people and animals, along with the Ebola virus and several species of undiscovered flesh eating bacteria.

None of that is confirmed of course, but it's a rather safe assumption.

Kitchen tables and chair, entertainment centers—basically anything that isn't covered in fabric that can absorb the aforementioned disgustingness is safe and I can kind of understand the appeal of the freeness.

But a rogue couch on the side of the road?

Unless you're planning on stripping it down to the foundation and reupholstering the dang thing, that's like picking up a hitchhiker 20 miles out from a prison.

Just like eating a 3-hour old hot dog shot out of a weenie gun, that's not the best idea, my friend.

I understand that I'm a bit biased seeing as how I love my couch more than a normal person should, but I would rather sit on a cold cement floor every day for the rest of my life than expose any part of my flesh to a used couch picked up on the side of the road.

Call me a snob, but just don't make me sit on that couch.

PART 2

PEOPLE

Cart Corral Corruptors

I write about grocery shopping a lot.

The reason for that is because a) I'm at the store a few times a week and b) I am an astute observer of human behavior and notice things others might not—like little kids sticking green beans up their noses and putting them back in the pile, old men in sweatpants suggestively fondling cucumbers, checkout belt divider creepers, etc.

Perhaps I need a new hobby, but then again, perhaps I just need my fresh produce and will sacrifice my sanity to bring home the broccoli.

At any rate, my latest public declaration is that there are two kinds of people in this world: 1) those who return carts to the cart corral and 2) a-holes.

Disclaimer: This observation excludes parents who might not want to leave their kids alone in the car to return the cart. I don't want to piss anyone off again. For that reason, you're excused.

But with that said, anyone else who refuses to return the cart to its home deserves to purchase and eat the boogery beans mentioned above.

Why?

Because shopping carts are provided for the convenience of customers. Cart corrals are provided for the specific purpose of controlling the carts so they don't roam free in the parking lot, creating an inconvenience that cancels out the aforementioned cart convenience.

These cart corrals are clearly marked and not hidden in some cart corral cave accessible only through a series of security measures and secret handshakes, and a shopping cart left to run amok can cause a great deal of damage and injury.

When it's windy, they blow around and are magnetically drawn to parked cars and elderly women who unknowingly take on the role of human bowling pins as they shuffle up to the doors to pick up their cat food and butterscotch candies.

Let's also mention that leaving a cart to find it's own way home often results in the cart camping out in a parking spot, a parking spot someone *(ahem)* will inevitably pull halfway into before realizing the cart is there and angrily backing out, pissing off people behind them.

It's a vicious cycle.

The fact is that carts cannot be trusted to return themselves to the cart corral. It takes a firm hand, determination and perhaps a few extra steps to see to it that they are put back where they belong. Before you know it, the cart jockey will come out with his little electric cart-picker-upper and round them all up to take back.

And while I hate to give out my secrets, I'll share a trick of the trade— park next to a cart corral.

This serves a couple of purposes, one being the fact that it's convenient to return your cart immediately upon shopping completion. But if you're anything like me and often find yourself wandering around the parking lot pretending you meant to walk up and down every aisle before settling back to your car, parking by a cart corral at least narrows down the options of where your car actually is.

You're welcome.

But the bottom line is the carts have a home. Help them find their home or be cast as a cart corral corruptor and feel much shame.

And for god's sake, wash your produce.

The Great Divide

The fact that the employees at my local grocery store know me and ask where I've been if I don't stop in every couple days gives you an indication of how often I'm at the store.

But don't worry.

This won't be about how I freak out when they're out of something I need—not want, but NEED people—or the fact that some cashiers don't know the difference between a banana and green beans.

No, this is about the checkout, specifically the plastic dividers.

I enjoy the grocery belt divider for the practicality and simplicity it provides.

Placed on the belt, it divides my order from the one in front and the one in back. There should be no confusion as to where one order starts and one order ends. If for some reason confusion does arise, it's not hard to clarify and say, "Oh, that's not my stuff."

However, there are still people who are entirely too concerned that the cashier will confuse their things with the next persons, protectively creating about two feet of extra "empty" grocery belt space between their order and the divider.

Intercom announcement to this person ahead of me: I did not load up my cart and assume that I could sneak 25 items to the end of your order, dupe you into paying for them and then follow you out to the parking lot to retrieve said items.

But with that said, I do have an issue with the people behind me from time to time. While I don't exhibit the behavior mentioned above and often *graciously* place the divider at the end of my order, this is apparently not enough for some people. No, instead of waiting for the cashier to move the belt along, they insist on using every single square inch of belt space up to the plastic divider.

43

This I can overlook, as it's their own bread they're squishing in an effort to unload their cart at warp speed.

What I can't overlook is when they insist on using every single square inch of personal space past the plastic divider, creeping up closer to me with their cart and sighing so heavily at the apparent lack of cashier expediency that it blows my coupons off the checkout stand.

Intercom announcement to this person behind of me: Regardless of how close you creep up or how many items you throw on the belt, you will be next—after me.

If you continue to creep up, I will pretend to go through my coupon keeper for an extraordinary amount of time, chit chat with the cashier and lift up the plastic divider and put it back down repeatedly under the guise of making room for a pack of gum I am actually just using as a prop to piss you off.

But because I'm all about solutions, I propose that instead of the grocery belt divider, we install a plastic divider *in the LINE* to keep the person behind me from creeping up and invading my bubble.

It could be like a shower curtain or one of those things you walk through at sporting events that simply lifts up and down when appropriate.

Now I realize this plastic divider could be symbolic of the way our society is divided and that unity can only be achieved when we remove these barriers, etc. People who think that are insane. I'm all about being friendly, but we need personal space—on the grocery belt and in the line.

Intercom announcement: Until they install these new plastic people dividers, please just back your shit up.

Unless, of course, you would like to pay for my produce. In that case, I welcome you with open arms and an open grocery belt.

Breaking News

I'm not really into the news.

While I think it's important to know what's going on, I'm okay with just grazing the surface with minimal awareness to the impending doom of the planet and how a trailer park manager won the lotto with a ticket he found in an opossum nest.

It's basically the same script each day with names, places and dates switched around like some perverted Mad Libs puzzle.

Of course the stories are different, but the premise is often the same. So while I've only been privy to a "behind the scenes" look at the news on one occasion—and it was a Saturday morning—I have to imagine the script looks something like this.

Breaking News!

Newscaster 1: Good morning! I'm Susie Sunshine.

Newscaster 2: And I'm Bob Boring. It's Monday and you're tuned into WXYZ, where we are the ONLY station to bring you the most EXCLUSIVE up-to-date news complete with witty banter and sexual tension between me and my co-host that can be cut with a dull butter knife.

N1: That's right, Bob. Ha, ha, ha! First off, the former mayor has been arrested on embezzlement charges from his current job at Popcorn Palace, but this isn't the first time he's been "popped" for that. We'll detail his criminal record coming up in 10.

N2: Thanks, Suze. There's also a warning out there today for anyone who has driven a car filled with gasoline, as it turns out that one false move could cause the car to explode. This is very important information, so be sure to tune into our 11 pm newscast 17 hours from now for the details.

N1: And we have some good news for you this morning about that giant lizard that was run over by a Segway driven by that 103-year-old man last week. Let's just say, he's "scaling" back to health.

N2: But first, let's throw it over to chief meteorologist, Guy Cloud, who is standing outside in the pouring rain and blowing winds. Guy!

(Throw it to weatherman standing outside in the pouring ran, holding onto his hat and umbrella while trying to talk into the microphone.)

Weatherman: Thanks guys! You don't need me standing outside in this horrible storm to tell you that it's raining outside, but I'll still tell you that it's raining outside and demonstrate this by standing outside in the rain.

As for the rest of the week, it's hard to pinpoint the exact weather that you can expect—although that's my job—so be sure to check back later tonight for your completely hypothetical 8 day forecast.

Remember, we're the MOST accurate storm team around! Back to you in the studio!

N1: What a Guy, ha ha!

N2: Indeed Suze, indeed. No one can rain on his parade! But bringing the focus back to us, coming up we'll tell you all about that semi-serious thing that happened and then include video of our reporter walking at the camera while talking and accenting scripted words with numerous hand gestures while ignoring everything behind them.

They will then interview someone off the street who is the least qualified to speak publically on the subject—or even be out in public at all—before offering up an introspective statement delivered for maximum impact.

N1: *(taking a sip from her coffee cup)* You're such a tease, Bob! I look forward to pretending to care.

N2: As do I, Suze. As do I. And now a word from our sponsors.

And…the Nun is Drunk

My mom brought home her nun friend from the old people's place to join us for Thanksgiving, so the day was entertaining…and exhausting.

Sister is a trip. Any time she leaves the home she gets a little excitable, especially when she gets into the wine, and Thursday was no exception.

Now there is no accurate way to describe her for a visual, but the closest I can come is to say she's a 5-foot-tall stripped down version of Cinderella's fairy godmother, but a little more troll-like.

Imagine darker gray hair, take out the wand, add a habit for certain situations and stick her on a motorized cart with a basket on the front that she usually drives the cart up and down the aisles of the home with the resident dog securely placed inside the basket.

Anyway, Sister was waiting outside in her oversized sweatshirt, sweatpants and sandals with socks when we picked her up from the home.

The five minute car ride revealed that she recently met a 30-year-old who wasn't married, which she—a nun—found odd. When it was pointed out that I was single and that Sister was a nun, this prompted her to declare that yes, she did actually know "shitload of 'normal' people" who weren't married, like her dentist and that one secretary at the doctor.

As we walked into the house, we were also told that at some point we had to go to the store—on Thanksgiving— to get her a new electric toothbrush.

Enter wine—not converted from water, but alcoholic nonetheless.

Sister tried to situate herself on the couch. This resulted in her falling in the couch crack, flipping the recliner part of the couch open and almost flying heels over head over the back. Recovered, she took a sip of her "spirit" and engaged my mom's husband in a conversation about cheese and Mexican saints.

I "helped" my mom in the kitchen, and by "helped" I don't mean fisting a bird, but rather making sure she had a beer.

The meal itself was full of stories.

Some I had heard before, others I hadn't about her traveling the world, accidentally legally changing her name to her "nun" name instead of the one she was given as an infant and how she knew she wanted to became a nun at 18, but that her mom wanted her to run the roads to make sure, at least going to prom with a boy.

"They were just one date things," she said. "I never tried to get laid."

"However," she continued, taking a sip of wine and leaving a mashed potato ring on her glass. "Some of the girls from the school used to go to the sand dunes and lay around with the boys. I was sent with them, but I don't like sand."

At that she picked up the turkey leg and continued gnawing on it like a carnivorous Catholic cavewoman.

"Is this the Super Bowl?" she asked as I turned up the Thanksgiving football game between Detroit and Green Bay. "Did you know people bet on these things? I heard sometimes the players lose on purpose and throw the matches. Is that what the Lions are doing?"

The next 30 minutes were spent explaining football to the buzzed nun, who kept claiming that her "craziness" was due to the eight mini peanut butter cups she had before dessert and not the wine.

"Are we the yellow pants or the gray pants?" she asked as she propped herself back on the couch, sipping her wine through a straw. "Ooh! Who has the ball—the 'G' or the 'D'? Are there any points out there? Can I take my wine home with me?"

She didn't forget about the toothbrush.

After once again implementing our makeshift Catholic catapult to get the nun in the truck, we made our way to the store, which was 10 minutes from closing. Sister honed in on what she wanted, grabbed the $7 Oral-B model from the ad and engaged the cashier in a conversation about her tartar issues and the dinner she just had.

As were walking out, a couple of men were walking in, which prompted Sister to proclaim with a huff, "The store is closing in five minutes, good sirs. I suggest you either hurry yourself up or come back again tomorrow, as that poor man hasn't even had dinner yet!"

"Can you believe how rude some people can be?" she asked as we boosted her back into the truck—again. "Now where are my peanut butter cups? Do you think the 'Gs' or the 'Ds' won the game? When can we do this again?"

Oh good lord.

Say a prayer for us all.

A Match for Martha

Martha Stewart, 71, told Matt Lauer on the "TODAY" show that she has trouble meeting men and admitted she attempted to *(unsuccessfully)* join Match.com.

Apparently she loves dating, but the questionnaire seemed impossible and so she's just going to keep looking on her own.

Well, I've never attempted online dating, but I think I could really help her out with this thing. After all, if weirdo Guy Fieri can find his Gal Fieri, there has to be hope left for Martha.

Username: Martha Stewart

Headline: Lifestyle guru, businesswoman, author, magazine founder and publisher, TV personality and domestic diva seeking companionship and snuggles with someone who appreciates the finer things in life.

Age: A spritely 71

Sign: Leo, which is perfect because I love my Himalayan cats!

Ethnicity: Whitest woman on the planet

Nickname: In prison it was "M. Diddy," but I would prefer to just go by Martha. Bygones!

Income: Well this is curious! My income range is not represented. No matter. I get by.

Religion: Cleanliness is next to godliness. Also, Dog is my co-pilot. Ha!

Relationships: One ex-husband and several ex-beaus, most notably a software billionaire and Anthony Hopkins, who I had to break it off

with after viewing that wretched film, "Silence of the Lambs." I was unable to avoid associating Hopkins with Hannibal Lecter, a man with absolutely no table manners or sense of proper etiquette.

Children: I've had many lovely dogs, cats and horses over the years, but I won't bore you with those details yet! However, if you're interested, my two blogging pups, Francesca and Sharkey, have created a photo gallery of all my pets.

Oh, and I have one daughter, Alexis.

Body Type: It depends on what I'm eating, but I prefer an Asti for a light-bodied wine and a Barbaresco for a full-bodied wine.

Celebrity Look-Alike: I've been told I could be a mix of that lovely woman who played Murphy Brown *(Candice Bergen)* and Diane Sawyer.

Smoke: Do you mean salmon? If so, yes. It can make a delightful appetizer when done correctly.

Drink: I love a whiskey sour with fresh juice or a mojito, but it has to be a purple basil mojito and the basil has to be cultivated from my own garden and tended to with painted garden tools.

Hobbies: Anything involving a hot glue gun—decoupage, scrapbooking, creating snow globes out of glass from upcycled chandeliers.

I enjoy knitting blankets from the hair of my prize-winning Chow Chows, baking "green" brownies with my pal Snoop Dogg/Lion out of cupcake tins I've created from paperclips and aluminum foil; building a billion-dollar empire and tweeting. I love the Twitter!

Who I'm Looking For: Someone who I can laugh with that knows they can use half a potato to unscrew a broken light bulb.

He should love animals, personal transformation and organized bed linens. There's something incredibly satisfying about opening up the linen closet to see not unholy chaos, but color-coded bundles neatly tied in a bow.

Note: Stockbrokers and actors who have portrayed cannibals need not apply.

I think it's pretty solid and can only imagine that the men would be lining up. And if all else fails, I'm pretty sure she could try Craig's List or get cast on "The Bachelorette."

Martha might just meet her match.

Senior Moments: Elvis

I realize that the job of words is to describe things, but sometimes there just aren't enough words to describe seeing nuns and senior citizens in wheelchairs dirty dancing with an Elvis impersonator on a sunny Saturday afternoon in September.

However, I will try in the latest "Senior Moments" installment.

This past weekend was the annual community carnival at the old people's place. The term "carnival" is a bit of a stretch, but they fill the huge parking lot and yard with booths of games for the kids, a very modest petting zoo, a bounce house *(for the kids, not the seniors)* and carts/tables of food, ice cream and drinks donated by local businesses.

Gram was having one of her good days, so mom and I wheeled her outside to mingle among the residents, employees and their families, goats, nuns wearing bright green "St. Ann's Carnival 2012" T-shirts over their habits and…Elvis.

Oh yes.

Elvis had left the building and set up shop on the makeshift stage. He was the real deal, resplendent in a white jumpsuit bedazzled with gold and silver gleaming in the late afternoon sun. His black hair hardly moved when the gentle breeze blew, and his sideburns accented his exposed chest hair of a similar hue.

While many of those in the audience were aware that this wasn't in fact the real Elvis, there was one senior friend who informed the Hunka Hunka Burning Love that she saw him in concert in 1957 and threw her panties on stage.

We were all just relieved that she didn't try and recreate that moment.

Elvis was actually awesome, although with his gyrating hips and plethora of "silk" scarves to give out to the ladies, I think at times he forgot that he was working a crowd of senior citizens, children and nuns.

One nun who had recently celebrated her 60th anniversary of sisterhood joined Elvis on stage for a rousing rendition of "Little Sister,"— dancing like she had been into the holy wine a wee bit too much — while Sister Judith grabbed the microphone stand and proceeded to dip left and right, a back-up singer to the King and the Lord for "Devil In Disguise."

When Elvis made his way towards Gram for a song, she joined in signing and dancing in her chair while the King placed a scarf around her neck. When asked later by a friend about this budding romance, she replied, "He's got business to take care of and I'm too tired right now. But that doesn't mean I won't be up for some fun yet tonight."

He continued making the rounds as each song came over the speakers, changing the words to fit the situation at times —"I really want one of those hot dogs" *(sung to "You Ain't Nothing But a Hound Dog")*—while the nuns continued to dance in the grass.

Add in a middle-aged woman who apparently thought she was at a karaoke bar after last call, an old guy who yelled, "what the hell are you doing?" when the microphone was thrust in his face and a dog dragging his ass across the grass in front of the stage, and that pretty much sums up the moment.

So as Elvis finished his rendition of "Rolling Down to St. Ann's," that's just what we did, rolling Gram back inside to the dining room to trade in her scarf for a "clothing protector" and food.

She is, after all, still the Queen.

For more in the Senior Moments series, you should probably buy my first book. There are quite a few gems stuck in there.

Exclusive Interview: Vanilla Ice

Scene: *An unprepared reporter interviews Robert Van Winkle, aka Vanilla Ice*

Sorry if I'm a bit flustered, but I'm actually not the person who was supposed to do this interview. The reporter who was assigned is apparently sick, although I suspect it's "the bar flu," if you know what I mean. Ha, ha.

I'm not so much a "reporter," per se, as a photographer for the pet fashion section of the paper. But I'm a team player. Plus, c'mon, you're Vanilla Ice! So I was all, "Will I ever stop? Yo, I don't know. Give me the address, and I'll go!"

I grew up listening to you, so big fan!

But enough about me, let's get to the questions. Of course, Dan, who was supposed to do the interview, wasn't able to give me the questions he was going to ask, so these are some I jotted down on the back of a napkin at Starbucks this morning. I didn't have a lot of time to prepare, but…

Oh my god! I just realized I was drinking ICED COFFEE when I was Googling you and preparing for this interview. Talk about meant to be!

So, one thing "off the record," as they say, before we really start. And this might have been influenced by the fact that I was drinking a mocha when I got the call to *do* the interview, but I think it's still of general interest: Do you prefer vanilla or chocolate?

I mean, the obvious answer would be vanilla, seeing as you're Vanilla Ice and all, but I'm thinking that name might just be symbolic of something more. Like maybe by "vanilla" you really meant "bland" in an ironic way, because obviously you're not bland at all. I didn't mean to imply that.

Anyway, I guess that's not important.

Questions. Let's see…sorry. I'm trying to read these scribbles here. The other day I wrote down "clean shower" and read it as "clean Steve" which would be really awkward if I was around someone named Steve!

Moving along.

Everyone knows "Ice Ice Baby" and that you worked with MC Hammer—how crazy were those pants, by the way?—but I'm supposed to ask you about *"The Vanilla Ice Project,"* a show you have on DIY where you guys, and I quote from the Internet, "pound nails and call the shots in this room-by-room renovation."

Is that like a metaphor for something or do you really build things? I once tried to assemble a bookcase from IKEA and almost glued my hands together, so maybe I should TiVo you, huh?

Anyway, they also told me to ask you about *"Vanilla Ice Goes Amish?"*

I thought maybe I wrote that down wrong and meant "danish," being in Starbucks and all, but I Googled it and found out you're going to have another show on DIY and, I quote, "immerse yourself in an Amish community in Ohio to learn how they do construction."

You do know that they don't have electricity right? What if they ask you to "play that funky music, white boy?" Are you going to be all, "To the extreme, I will pump that butter handle. Light up the room with a waxy homemade candle?"

I just came up with that! If you use it, let me know!

OK, I'll guess I'll just watch and see.

But I have to know… do you ever walk into a room and say something like "Hey, I'm back!" and your friends and family are like, "With a brand new invention?" And then you chime in with, "Something, grabs a hold of me tightly" and you all have a good laugh?

Well, no matter. What's that? Our time is done? Bummer. I had some really good questions coming up. I'll guess I'll just look for you on TV and I thank you for your time.

Word to your mother!

My Batman

I deal with a lot of companies for part of my job that bank their success on the licensing of Hollywood trends, so needless to say, superheroes have been everywhere the past couple of years.

This got me thinking, which we all know isn't my superpower.

Yes, it would be nice to hook up with a Man of Steel that could leap tall buildings, but let's be honest. Who really wants to be around someone that needs to find an actual phone booth to change clothes?

Impossible and impractical, not to mention disgustingly germy.

So instead I have created my own version of the superheroes I would like to see wandering the streets and helping to better mankind—or just me.

Spider-Man

So a skinny gentleman gets bit by a genetically modified spider and gains spider-like abilities that he must use to fight evil. I've been bitten by a spider and all that I gained was a huge painful welt and the inherent paranoia that suddenly spiders WERE EVERYWHERE and I must use a sandal to smash up the evil.

Instead, I would like a Spider-Man to instinctively sweep in every time the arachnid nemesis attempts to tip-toe his way into my house and I have to try to "save" it with a piece of paper and a cup to shoo it into before freaking out and just stepping on it.

Batman

Forget Bruce Wayne and the passive-aggressive Robin. All I'm asking for is a hot baseball player. The end.

Iron Man

A rich guy has an accident, is forced to build an armored suit and decides to use its technology to fight against evil. Really. An armored suit. That will really come in handy when it's 103 degrees in Michigan with 80 percent humidity.

Instead of that scenario, I want an Iron Man to actually come and do ironing. This is the part of the program in which faithful readers remember how much I love ironing and I tell those who are new here that I don't exactly love ironing. Or iron, for that matter.

The Avengers

I don't need a group of superheroes trying to stop Thor's disgruntled brother from taking over the Earth. I would just like this group of intimidators to avenge the murder of a few of my plants as a result of the woodchuck who has broken through the impenetrable fortress I've created around my garden.

The furry bastard must go.

Avengers unite.

Catwoman

Apparently a woman with the speed, reflexes and senses of a cat walks a thin line between criminal and hero. Hmmm…this is one I could get behind. I'm not fast and my reflexes are comparable to those of a sleeping sloth, but I feel like I might possess a few cat-like senses— namely the fact that I can be anti-social, possessive of food and distracted by colorful things.

However, I can't explain why my cat would prefer to sleep on a shelf and not the cushy leopard print cat bed that's available to her instead.

I suppose that's why we need superheroes.

Employee of the Month

Scene: *Job interview at Hypothetical Honesty Office & Co.*

Important Company Person: Hello! Thank you for coming in for this interview today. Your resume is quite impressive.

Applicant: Thank you for inviting me! No one is posting jobs that I'm qualified for, so my resume is a complete work of fiction that highlights my creative writing and improvisational skills.

ICP: Indeed! Now let's get down to business. We want someone who is willing to work hard for a small amount of money so that the higher ups can work less and make a fortune. We could hire anyone we wanted to come in and do this generic office position, but we want someone with practical skills, so I'm going to ask you a few important questions. Ready?

A: Does this involve a drug test?

ICP: No.

A: Then yes, let's begin.

ICP: You have CEO listed on your resume. Can you explain what those duties entailed?

A: Well, CEO means "Cleaner of External Objects" to me. And as CEO, I always replace the empty roll of paper towel in the kitchen or bathroom, as I know that's a hard skill to master. I also place my dirty coffee cup *IN* the sink and then wash it instead of placing it *NEXT* to the sink and leaving it for an imaginary maid.

And at my last job, I had to fix the running toilet in the office bathroom. Does that make me a hero? Not for me to say. But probably.

ICP: Impressive and noted—with a smiley face! Now it's a proven fact that the first 10 minutes of any conference call are spent watching people try and figure out how to set up the conference call. How do you deal with a) phones and b) meetings.

A: I'm more terrified of a ringing phone than I am of a fire alarm, so I let all calls go directly to a voicemail that I never check. And any invitations to attend a webinar or meeting longer than an hour will result in me decoupaging a flask for my desk or faking my death.

ICP: Look at you, Martha Stewart with your crafts! Next question. The other day I yelled, "Don't you know who I am?" at the printer. Apparently it does, which would be why it jammed. How would handle that scenario?

A: I would do a little karate yell while trying to unjam said copy machine. Not sure it would help, but I'm feeling pretty confident it would.

ICP: Confidence is key. We want our employees to be as assertive as the Adobe Acrobat update reminders.

A: And there was one time I was feeling a bit overwhelmed and then "Eye of the Tiger" popped into my head. Long story short, I weaponized my stapler.

ICP: Random, but impressive, as I often use music to soothe me as well. When a pen runs out, I like to sing "Circle of Life" ceremoniously before placing it gently in the trash. We live in crazy times, don't we? Speaking of crazy, how do you deal with coworker interaction?

A: Well, my 30s have been less about "finding myself" and more about "finding ways to avoid awkward chit-chat." So every Monday I would handle general "How was your weekend?" inquiries by making flashcards stating: "Weekend was great!" "Weather is wonderful!" "Can't believe it's Monday!" It would cut down on talking by 25 percent.

ICP: Brilliant! I love that idea! It would not only increase productivity and profits, but also reduce stress. Of course you know I will claim it as my own and never give you the credit.

A: Understood. I will also passive aggressively update my Facebook status with a vague reference to that fact.

ICP: I wouldn't expect anything less! Welcome aboard.

So You Joined a Gym

If you belong to a gym, you know the New Years crowd that descends upon the facility. Machines will be busy, the parking lot will be full and for a good two months the place will swell with momentary motivation, testosterone and a lingering scent of body odor.

Those who stick around will soon become initiated with certain people and unspoken rules of the gym. If you're new to the gym scene, here's a stereotypical primer.

1. Some women will primp before the gym and then walk around without actually lifting a weight. Remind them that telling everyone about their fitness plan won't make them healthier unless they're doing it door to door — they love that.
2. With men, you may see Hammer pants and fanny packs paired stylishly with weight belts and wrestling shoes. Do not be alarmed! This is apparently a conscious decision on the part of the "bodybuilder" and any attempts to suggest otherwise will be frowned upon — they will not love that.
3. Outbursts and primal grunting are perfectly accepted and often encouraged with statements like, "You got this!" and "Lift that shit!" Interject your own encouragement like "Hugs not drugs!"— they love that.
4. Chit chat may occur, but only when the other person is resting in between sets. If you are in the middle of an exercise, plan on someone asking you a question completely unrelated and irrelevant.
5. If you're anything like me, Sundays at the gym will consist of 50 percent of people talking about how hung-over they are, 49 percent of people pretending to listen and you.
6. People will be wearing iPods and the like, oblivious to the fact that if they sing, we can hear them. Join in — it's fun for all!
7. People will write things down. They will do one set of pull-downs and after flexing in the mirror to admire the results of those eight reps of awesomeness, they will record it in their little notebook. Ask them if they're writing a haiku — the look on their face will be priceless.
8. Men will voluntarily shave things women hate to shave.

9. Most gyms have the hard core guys that know days of the week not by Monday or Tuesday but by Leg Day and Shoulder Blow-Out Bonanza sessions. Most gyms also have a group of older women that meet in the morning and get most of their exercise from running their mouths and fueling the rumor mills. Do not mess with their coffee.

10. Do not stare directly at someone using the inner/outer thigh machine who is wearing shorts. It's like staring at the sun—you will not love this.

11. There will be stalkers. People will hover around and wait for your piece of equipment or cardio machine despite the fact that there are a plethora of other options they could be using. Make loud noises or begin singing to buy yourself a few extra sets.

12. People in the parking lot will also stalk you for a closer parking spot, even though that defeats the purpose of going to the gym. Chances are it's not a cardio day, and therefore not something written down in the notebook.

13. And finally, the sweatier and grosser you get at the gym, the more people you will run into when you stop to the store immediately after. However, ducking in and out of the aisles with your cart and sprinting to the register can also count as cardio.

It's really a win all around.

Perpetuating Stereotypes

Everyone blogs for different reasons, but like anything else there are certain stereotypes that exist. While they most certainly don't hold true for everyone, there's a reason the stereotype developed—because it's true in one way or another.

So without further ado, I present my list of stereotypical bloggers.

Mommy Bloggers

Forget Bigfoot. The most elusive creature on the planet is a mommy blogger who never mentions wine—needing wine, drinking wine, cooking with wine so they can drink *and* eat the wine, etc.

They'll tell you they're doing all this drinking in sweatpants and dirty shirts because they haven't had time to shower in three days. However, they have the time to take a picture of their dirty house/adorable children that make them lose their mind, blog about not having time to shower and then promote their daily blog post—which is usually some sort of infographic— on Twitter/Facebook 212 times a day.

They also run in a pack mentality, so beware. Do not incite the Mommy Blogger or say anything as I just did above. They will attack. Then drink wine.

The Apologetic Blogger

About 75 percent of this blogger's posts involve him or her apologizing for not posting more often. At one point this blogger probably posted more frequently before life suddenly got in the way and blogging fell by the wayside.

Note: While readers might have been concerned, the world went on without your posts. No apologies for living your life.

Food Bloggers

Posts from these culinary paparazzi will start out with something like, "THIS just happened" or "Look what I made you!" followed by a picture of something they didn't eat because it took them 57 tries to perfect the shot before plastering text of the recipe name over the image so people can "pin" it.

You might go there for a recipe, but you will end up with a 500-word backstory about the creation of the "best thing EVER" and 12 pictures of the dish in various stages of spilling before getting to the ingredients and reader comments about how they're "drooling" and/or "licking the screen" and "trying to stab the picture with a fork."

The Expert

This self-proclaimed guru will tell you how to succeed at blogging and social media despite any credible research, credentials or data to support their theories other than spending 10 hours a day online. They often sound like a used car salesman with SEO keywords and links back to other "expert" social media bloggers.

Don't forget to tweet, Facebook and share all their posts.

Fiction Bloggers

A visit to this blog cannot be random/infrequent and still make sense, as they most often post pieces of whatever fiction they're working on at the time. It's like opening up a book to a random chapter and expecting things to make sense.

Thoughtful and endlessly tortured, these bloggers are always writing the Next Great American Novel and searching for "concrit," or constructive criticism. They join various writing groups of people who are also writing the Next Great American Novel and together in gangs they will often solicit your vote for whatever contest they're entering to help them become the author of the Next Great American Novel.

Health and Fitness Bloggers

Even though health and fitness are the focus of the blog, it often seems like a cult. They have their own language that includes things like "WOD" *(Workout of the Day)* and "WIAW" *(What I Ate Wednesday)* and seem to sustain their energy for hours of strenuous exercise through protein pancakes, odd Greek yogurt concoctions *(sent to them by sponsors)* and "healthy" versions of things that in no way resemble the "thing."

Note: You did not make "healthy" chicken nuggets out of rice. You made rice in the shape of a nugget.

They're called "motivational" in the comments and prove it by posting endless inspirational posters and self-portraits and ending every conversation with a hashtag #fitfanatic #paleoprincess

Humor Bloggers

Easily distracted by shiny things, these neurotic bloggers excel in shorter formats like Twitter and Facebook where one-liners are easier to form than whole blog posts. However, they still blog to a) make people laugh and b) mask their disappointment and insecurity over never getting "discovered" or picked to co-write an episode of "30 Rock" with Tina Fey.

They're frustrated, but they laugh to keep from crying. And a lot of them were probably dropped on their head as a kid. There can be no other good explanation.

---

*Now remember that there are dozens of funny, rational moms who blog and talented food bloggers, for example. We're generalizing here, people.

Except with the humor bloggers.

That part is mostly all true.

PART 3

(Going) PLACES

I Was Just Leaving

I'm really not anti-social. It's just that I'm pro-doing things by myself.

While I enjoy people to a certain extent, it's simply that I enjoy them in small doses and preferably online where I can pick and choose my level of social interaction—and simply click away when they annoy me.

And because I do have the choice, I will click away instead of dedicating this post to how social media has made me anti-social.

You're welcome.

But when I'm forced into a *(seemingly fun)* social situation such as a holiday party or drinks with friends, I can openly admit that I'm more charismatic and enjoyable than one may expect. It's like a social spark is lit, and if encouraged—or sipping my one drink of the night—I can shamelessly own the room until I leave.

There's the catch—the exit.

You see, I never know how to properly leave a social situation, but I always want to go. Quickly. There is about a maximum two hour window, at which point I'm like Cinderella running down the stairs towards her pumpkin carriage before the stroke of midnight.*

Just sub in a pair of running shoes and a Chevy Blazer for the glass slipper and carriage, but when it comes to the cleaning and talking to small animals, me and Cindy are practically twins.

I don't know how to tell people that I only want to stay for an hour or so, as I don't think "most people" would understand. "Most people" look forward to going out for hours and socializing, whereas I tend to get a little too excited when I am relieved of any social obligation that might leave me held against my will for an undisclosed amount of time.

So I make excuses both as to why I'm not going or why I have to leave, simply because I think it's easier than going and saying, "This hour has been fun, but now I would like to go home, wash off this coat of mascara, turn on the game and crash on the couch. Good night now."

That just seems rude.

If it's a large event with tons of people, I can usually say a polite goodbye to the host and slip out unnoticed at a time of my choice. If it's a small event though, I have to plan my escape accordingly and have a contingency plan securely in place.

The thing is, it doesn't even have to be an event. It can just be a normal visit to a friend or my grandma that requires some sort of half-truth about how I have laundry in the dryer or that I have to go to the store, simply because I always feel the need to bail at some point 10 minutes short of a socially acceptable amount of time.

But in my defense, I do go to the store a lot.

While I know that making an appearance is often good enough—and I do usually enjoy myself for that hour or so—the stress of the exit execution often drives me to write posts about the stress of the exit execution.

See how exhausting this is?

I just thought you should know that if you ever invite me anywhere, you have about an hour of quality time before I'll start looking like a claustrophobic cat. Depending on your tolerance for socializing with me, an hour might be just the right amount of time.

Anyway…well, this is a bit awkward.

I'll just say this post has been fun, but now I would like to go home, wash off this coat of mascara, turn on the game and crash on the couch.

Good night now.

I Can Drive 55

Even if I've done nothing wrong, my heart still jumps into my throat any time I either see a police car in my rearview mirror or drive by one running radar on the side of the road.

I have nothing but respect for law enforcement—various family members/friends are cops—but when I'm driving, it scares the crap out of me to see them on the road.

There's really no reason for this paranoia.

I am normally a very law-abiding driver, give or take a few road rage urges from time to time, and I've only had one ticket in all my years of *(legally)* driving. It came when I was in high school after I unsuccessfully argued that there was no way my piece of shit Ford Escort could actually go 70 mph without spontaneously combusting.

The officer didn't seem to care.

Aside from that $80 misunderstanding, I was also pulled over two other times in college in the same exact spot in the same week—both times when I was skipping class, which should have been a sign. But that's not important, as no ticket was issued either time.

However, now every time I pass a cop and I'm actually going the speed limit, I feel like I should get some sort of extra credit or build up a stack of bonus points that I can cash in on those days I might *not* be going the speed limit, hypothetically speaking, of course.

This hasn't caught on yet, but there's still hope.

I bring this up because there has been an interesting development recently concerning the speed limits on a few of the roads in my area. They have raised them without telling anyone, and by "anyone," of course I mean me.

There are a couple stretches of road that have been set at 35 mph and 45 mph respectively for as long as I can remember, and quite honestly, that was kind of a ridiculous expectation. Most people—not me, of course—went 45 in the 35 and at least 50 in the 45.

These stretches of road were also popular speed traps.

But as I was driving along the other day, I noticed that people were flying by me a bit more than normal. After mentally performing a citizen's arrest, I caught sight of the speed limit sign, one that seemed to have gained 10 mph since the last time I took note.

What? How is this not broadcast on the news? Did I miss a memo?

It seems the powers that be either tired of having to hear bullshit excuses from people being pulled over in this area or finally realized the ridiculousness of their "speed suggestions" and changed the speed limits. This delighted me, not because I want to speed, but because it just seems to make more sense.

But the truth?

Now that the law has been changed, I feel like a total rebel badass and purposely go that route at times just so I can legally zoom down the streets a good 10 mph faster than I've been able to do in the past.

People who haven't been as observant as yours truly stare at me as I whiz by, most likely praying I get caught in the speed traps so often set on this stretch.

But little do they know that I will NOT be caught in this trap, as I am simply abiding by the new speed suggestions. Yes, now I can legally drive 55 without crapping kittens* if I pass a cruiser poised on the side of the road sticking something that resembles a hairdryer out of his/her window.

*OK. That's not true. My heart will still jump into my throat, but that kind of detracts from the badass-ness I am trying to exhibit here. I was born to be wild.

Driving Aunt Mable

I've conducted research in a few different states and have come to the conclusion that riding in a taxi should be considered an extreme sport.

Most cab drivers not only drive defensively, but get defensive when anyone goes <u>only</u> a minimum of 10 mph over the speed limit or fails to fly through yellow lights and stop signs.

But looking past the germ factor and high risk of whiplash and death, I actually kind of enjoy taking a cab when I travel. Not to generalize, but most big city drivers are foreign and have a really interesting story about coming to America from a war-torn town to escape and find a better life.

I'm nosy and I ask.

That's what made my last cab ride to the airport in Dallas a bit interesting, as instead of the skinny guy from India who offered me sunflower seeds and chanting music earlier in the week, I had Aunt Mable.

When the valet at the hotel opened up the door to the minivan taxi, I was presented with an extremely large black woman dressed as if she were going to the prom, squeezed in behind her seatbelt like a pillow wrapped in twine.

She swiveled her head back to look at me, large rainbow-colored hoop earrings swinging side to side, and pointed with a florescent colored nail. "You ready to ride with Aunt Mable, sweetheart?"

I'm not going to lie. I was a little excited, as this one seemed like she was fun.

I was putting on my seatbelt when Aunt Mable turned down the gospel music to say, "Sweet baby Jesus! Tell me you buckled up back there. Safety first, sweetheart, safety first. Mm-hmm."

This is what we call "foreshadowing."

As I settled in and we pulled away, it became clear that according to Aunt Mable, the Dallas highways at 6:30 am on a Sunday morning magically transform into the Autobahn. While I couldn't see it from the back, I imagined a pudgy lead foot stuffed into a sequined pump like a sausage putting the pedal to the metal.

We quickly zoomed to 60, 70 and then 80 mph through the darkness, making small talk as the Whataburgers and John Deere dealerships flew by in a blur. I found out she was from Dallas and "praise sweet baby Jesus," had six kids.

After breaking the sound barrier, we arrived at the airport. Since my airline had three terminals and I was unsure which one I was at, she decided we would stop and ask the skycap because, "You choose to ride with Aunt Mable, you get the whole package, sweetheart. No ma'am, you not gonna wander around that airport like a lost puppy."

So after the skycap directed us to my terminal and I paid, she handed me my receipt and a butterscotch candy from a bag she kept in between the seats—along with a fire extinguisher, an air freshener and what looked to be a Harlequin romance novel.

"You're on your own with the bags," Aunt Mable informed me. "That ain't part of the package sweetheart, as the good lord done blessed me with good taste but a bad hip!"

So I grabbed my bags from the back and watched her cab speed off into the rising sun like a superhero bumblebee before preparing to strip down for my walk through security.

Safety first, sweetheart, safety first.

Pump It Up

People in Michigan are prone to complain about two things—the weather and gas prices, but for good reason.

Our weather can be ridiculous, and we're known to have some of the highest gas prices in the country. So when it's 95 degrees or we have 100 inches of snow and gas is $4.10/gallon, it's best to stick to safe topics like religion or politics.

But with that said, gas is a necessary evil. Seeing as I can take a seemingly routine vehicular activity and turn it into an issue of sorts, it's not a surprise that pumping gas is no exception.

I really don't remember a time when we could pull up to a pump and have a smiling face come out to fill 'er up.

Today I pull up to one of the pumps—careful not to pull up too far, as to prevent someone from using the one in front of me—and if someone did approach my car, smiling or not, I would lock the doors and then either prepare my awesome ninja skills or start the car and drive away.

Because it's all pre-pay now, I usually opt for the pay at the pump option. At this point, the cashier's voice comes over the intercom like some sort of omniscient gasoline god and greets me and I'm left wondering what I should do. Do I say "hi" back, not knowing if they can hear me but well aware that I just shouted, "I'm fine! Thanks for asking!" out to a semi-vacant parking lot?

Forget the meaning of life. These are the questions that need to be asked.

But there are times my card can't be read for whatever reason and I have to go in the store and manually pay for the gas like it's 2010. The cashier that greeted me so warmly before will ask me what pump I'm at and then immediately express complete annoyance at the fact that I'm not prepared and have no idea, opting instead to point to my car at the pump.

Knowing I need him more than he needs me, I smile warmly and silently regret my decision not to carry on a whole conversation at the pump via intercom just moments before.

The attendant then *(deeply sighs and)* activates the pump, at which point I begin the walk of shame back to my Blazer and proceed with the process at hand, making a mental note of what pump I'm at and carrying on a compensatory conversation with the attendant via an intercom that I'm 99 percent certain is no longer on.

Better safe than sorry, and talking to yourself at the pump will deter any weirdos from approaching your car.

But sometimes actually going into the store and pre-paying for gas is quite helpful, as it will stop the pump at an exact amount and I can attempt to clean my windshield during the pumping process. If forced to pump on my own, I'm pretty sure I spend an extra $10 just trying to get the pump to end on an even amount.

Plus, one day last week the cashier jokingly carded me when I was forced to go inside to buy gas. He was about 112 years old with five teeth, but we're going steady now—until he brings up the weather.

This is Your Captain Speaking

Here's the thing about flying.

It's the ultimate loss of control.

Whereas someone driving you around in a car is theoretically more dangerous than someone flying you around in a plane — especially if it's a cab driver, as good lord they're freakishly fearless — at least I can bail out of the car or choose the radio station.

This is not an option in an airplane.

So you basically board the big metal bird and trust that the dude in the captain's hat had his Starbucks and not a fight with his wife and/or girlfriend before coming to work and navigating a gazillion ton airplane 30,000 feet into the sky.

The captain does often try to connect with you on some level, although I think they overdo it a bit and supply the passengers with completely unnecessary information.

The general overview of the flight, weather conditions, etc. are all great facts to have, but they were probably already mentioned by the flight attendants before they plowed through the aisles with their metal carts full of juice and water.

But why do we always need to know exactly how high we're flying multiple times throughout the flight?

"Ladies and gentleman, this is your captain speaking. We're currently at an altitude of 17,000 feet and should reach our cruising altitude in about 14 minutes and 33 seconds."

I'm not sure what to do with this information, and let's be honest. No one is sitting in their tiny little seat with their tray tables in the upright position logging the altitude of the flight like a fan keeps the box score at a ballgame. All most people care about it making sure the plane is flying high enough not to hit the trees and buildings below.

If they're going to interrupt my attempt at a nap or try and distract me from the fact that three birds just flew through the engine, they should present passengers with more interesting facts about the person who could potentially turn the plane into a flaming inferno of death.

"Ladies and gentleman, this is your captain speaking. Did you know that after graduating from flight school, I celebrated by streaking through the streets of Barcelona in nothing but a red banana hammock?"

"I don't mean to brag, but I've gone 465 days on the job without an accident or 'incident.'"

"If I had to choose my favorite meal, it would be lasagna with homemade garlic bread. I eat it before every flight, you know, just in case."

I would even settle for interesting random facts, kind of a "tweet-like" account of what's really going on up in the air.

"If you choose to use the lavatory in the next 15 minutes, you will be emptying your bladder at exactly the same altitude as Mauna Kea, the world's tallest mountain."

"My co-pilot wants me to tell you that he just finished a crossword puzzle in ink, if anyone's looking for a hero."

"Woo-hoo! Conditions are great and this kick-ass tail wind means we're going to arrive early. This thing is like a manic hummingbird on speed today!"

I'm still not sure what I do would do with that information either, but I can guarantee I could have written a much more entertaining blog post than this.

At any rate, it *is* nice that they thank us for choosing their airline and acknowledge the fact that we had other options, even if we really didn't seeing as there was probably only one flight in and out of our destination for the next month.

Still, I suppose they try, and with that I will say:

"Ladies and gentlemen, this is your blogger speaking. I would like to thank you for choosing 'Abby Has Issues' today, as I know you had other options. Please be sure to check back again for all your future neurotic needs."

Timing Is Everything

This will come as a surprise to no one, but I always have to be early or at least on time.

This is often to my detriment, as 98 percent of the population is apparently not this way, which means is I end up hurrying to wait. This in turn causes extreme frustration, occasional cursing and the creation of several voodoo dolls. Yet I still insist on being on time for things.

Why?

Because, well, OCD and schedules, *but more importantly*, because it's simply respectful.

On a professional note, I'll just say that deadlines are not suggestions people. You are not a special snowflake. That sense of entitlement and lack of respect is rude and frustrating.

In my personal life, I feel the same way. If you tell me to be ready at 6, please be there at 6. While I understand things happen, making me wait 30 minutes or more is grounds for violent behavior. By the time you show up, I will be too bitter and annoyed that you couldn't get your shit together to be fun.

That will be your fault.

This is also why I always prefer to be the picker-upper and not get picked up. At least I can sit in your driveway and honk the horn like the crazy person you have forced me to be.

This annoyance is most prevalent in appointments—doctors, dentists, hairstylists, etc. Again, I understand things happen, but there is no good reason for them to happen every single time.

But I think dentists and doctors have figured out we're annoyed with this and have devised their own plan.

The time spent in the waiting area has been cut down significantly, and at first I was excited to be called back to my own little room rather quickly.

However, this was before I realized I was put there so when I freaked out over waiting 45 minutes it would be in the privacy of an exam room and not the public waiting area.

Side note: Please don't tell me to read a magazine, as those things are like public Petri publications full of germs and nastiness. You might as well lick a toilet seat.

But I've devised my own revenge.

I fill the time looking for fun little things I can take as a memory of my excursion. This obviously can't be done somewhere like a hair salon where going through the drawers and taking bobby pins and shower caps would be frowned upon.

But if you're stuck in an exam room for more than 40 minutes, you can legally take things like Band-Aids with cool cartoons characters, cotton balls and stickers given to good little patients.*

*I read that on the Internet—right after I wrote it—so it must be true.

Inevitably the same nurse who has avoided me for 40 minutes will walk in the one second I'm looking for a tongue depressor I can make into a little stick man, but whatever.

At that point I no longer feel like talking about whatever I went there to talk to them about anyway, even if my head is about to fall off, so why not at least walk out with an art project?

I know, I know.

Patience, not petty theft, but if everyone would just stick to a schedule—*preferably mine*—I wouldn't be faced with this problem.

Remember that at the end of the day, it's about respect.

So if you insist in being late on multiple occasions, there's a good chance I will either sit in your driveway and blast the horn or steal your cotton balls.

That will be your fault.

Timing is everything.

Brush It Off

For many people who live in a state that experiences winter—and I don't mean 50 degrees one day out of the year, California friends—snow is inevitable.

That means that for those of us who don't keep their vehicle in a covered garage because the weirdos that built their house 60 years ago failed to equip the garage door with the tools to be automatic, scraping the ice and snow off said vehicle is pretty much a regular thing.

It's also almost a science.

I have a remote car starter that I can activate from the warmth of my house, but it's an automatic car starter—not an automatic "scrape all the crap off your entire snow-covered vehicle including the roof and the back end"-type thing.

There's still quite a bit of work to be done.

- Hit the starter so the defroster can begin its work.
- Dress as warmly as possible with coat, hat and gloves. Take off my gloves when I remember I can't tie my boots with big gloves on.
- Gloves off, I tie my boots and make sure to tuck my pants into my socks so I don't a) lose my sock when I take off my boots and b) get snow stuck in my boot.
- Put gloves back on. Struggle to unlock and open the door.
- Take gloves off, open door, head outside and put gloves back on.
- Get distracted and shovel the walkway.
- Grab snow brush out of my car.
- Brush the burst of snow off the driver's seat that falls in upon opening the door. Every. Single. Time.
- Start with brushing the snow off the roof.
- Curse the wind that is blowing the snow directly back into my face and continue to brush what I can reach, leaving an icy unreachable island in the middle of the roof.
-

- Move on to the side and back windows. Feel proud that I remembered to brush off the lights and my license plate, both caked with ice.
- Prepare plan of attack for the windshield. Sometimes there's only a dusting of ice that the defroster can tackle alone. However, some mornings the ice is so thick that I need the strength of a roided up rhino to scrap that stuff off.
- While strategizing, a large gust of wind will blow through.
- Notice that half of the snow from the hood of my car is now lodged between my sock and my boot.
- Wonder why I'm living in such a frigid climate, how the bastard groundhog keeps his job and yell at the garage as it mocks me.
- Take rage out on scraping off ice.
- Scrape, scrape, scrape…still scraping.
- Lift up frozen windshield wipers.
- Scrape, curse, scrape, curse, scrape…still scraping, still cursing.
- Realize the defroster is starting to kick in and actually helping me out.
- Quit cursing.
- Get hit in the face with the snow from the roof that I couldn't reach with the brush.
- Resume cursing.
- Decide it's "clean enough" and walk back towards the house.
- Shovel the walkway again before struggling to unlock and open the door.
- Take gloves off, open door, head inside and take off boots.
- Build small igloo out of snow that's removed from my boot.
- Show cat small igloo made from snow that's removed from my boot.
- Clean up bloody scratches on my arms from less-than-thrilled cat.
- Decide it's not worth leaving home.
- Turn off car.
- Make tea.
- Spike tea.
- Count down the days until spring.

PART 4

THINGS

A Raw Deal

Now I don't want to curse anything, especially seeing as I haven't heard back yet, but I think there's a really good chance my ship might have finally come in, my friends.

While I was perusing Craig's List, I came upon an ad that, well, I guess I should let it speak for itself. *

*Reprinted exactly as listed, despite grammatical errors that make me twitchy. But with fate, one can't be picky!

Hello,

We are hiring for a one-time professional model for one evening. We will be celebrating a birthday and we will have Sushi Chefs carve the most delicate and fattiest Tuna there is right before our eyes, we'll be pouring the most satisfying sake, and all we need left is YOU. A beautiful, yet professional model who we will eat SUSHI off of.

It's simple. You come to our designated location. You undress. Get one the table. We will cover your goodies with bamboo leaves so no it's not full nude. Our chefs who we also hired will be preparing sushi and plating directly on your body. We will eat and dine for approx no more than 2 hours. It will be awesome! If you're interested please email back with an attached photo of yourself.

Pay is negotiable but we will start at $100/hr + travel expenses/accommodations, heck you can take the leftover sushi home with you!

I was a little hesitant at first, but the fact they offer to cover my "goodies" with bamboo was a nice gesture. However, what really sold me was that not only will it be "awesome," but heck! I can take the leftover sushi home with me!

Never mind the fact I'm not a professional model — details, details — I felt compelled to reply with a couple questions I had.

Konnichiwa!

I came across your Craig's List ad for a sushi model and before I send you my picture, I was wondering if you could answer a couple of questions.

Because I'm rather large in the chest region, how will that work when I'm lying down? My large breasts will most likely flop to the sides, and I would hate for any of the expensive sushi product to be wasted. I was thinking that perhaps each boob could be propped up on the sides with a chopstick?

Also, have you considered what might happen if the model were to sneeze? Do you have a backup supply of sushi in case this incident occurs?

It's not that I'm prone to sneezing, but the last time I was used as a human buffet, pepper was spilled. I don't think I have to tell you how messy it can be when a baked potato body bar experiences a violent eruption! I'm still picking chives out of my hair (Don't worry though. Those will be gone by the time I show up for this event.)

I am rather tall, and so my figure would make an excellent table for your meal. In addition, I also have an "innie" belly button that could be used for a wasabi holder or Sake shooter, if needed.

If you can guarantee that it will be no longer than two hours—I have a bladder the size of a Cheerio. Ha!—that it will indeed be "awesome" and that I will be supplied with a Styrofoam cooler to take home the extras (I only need the veggie option,) I would love to be considered for this position.

Thanks so much!

Truth In Advertising

I'm not one of those fancy people that has a DVR to record shows without commercial interruption. This means that when I have the TV on and I'm doing other things at the same time instead of sitting there to watch the show I was waiting to sit down and watch, I am exposed to advertising.

While some commercials are highly entertaining—I could watch the Slowsky's all day—most of them are annoying and last so long that I've forgotten what show I was watching and vow to never buy their product.

But in the spirit of expanding my worldly knowledge to dispense among the dozens of you who flock to this blog, I decided to share some insight.

What I've Learned from Watching TV Commercials

- I have a majority of side effects of multiple prescription drugs that I've never even taken.
- Men are all balding, irresponsible and only respond to sex, food and things that explode. They can't be trusted to buy anything without their wives or girlfriends, but they can however use a grill while wearing an apron and smiling.
- Lipstick is made of some cement-like substance that will never come off until you tell it to.
- Melted cheese must be stretched out before consumption and a frozen dinner is apparently the secret ingredient to spicing up a romantic evening.
- Outback Steakhouse is really, really Australian.
- When a family gets a new luxury SUV, the first thing they do is take it off road and drive through one-lane mountain passes and water-covered roadways at breakneck speed.
- Everyone laughs when they're eating candy or wearing a tampon.
- On that note, it's perfectly acceptable to pull out an unused tampon and show it off in a group setting.

- Kids don't watch TV— they watch toasters — and they find it fun to patiently wait for their Pillsbury Toaster Strudel.
- Every one of my local news stations is the most accurate, watching out for me more than anyone else and willing to put their lives on the line to bring me the news.
- Senior citizens with bowel and bladder problems spend part of every day in tennis whites.
- In order to get rich, I need to get attacked by a dog or injured in an automobile accident, in the workplace or through a hospital's negligence so I can sue *(and the lawyer can afford to not make his/her own commercials.)*
- No one can back their car out of a garage or driveway without incident.
- All breakfast foods aimed at children now contain "More Fiber!" than it takes to fill an industrial silo, which leads me to believe all children are constipated.
- Speaking of that, when a group of female friends get together they spend all their time talking about constipation or eating yogurt, which is apparently the key to fulfilling their innermost serenity *(the yogurt, not constipation.)*
- Bacon and diarrhea have the same manic PR person, as almost every commercial includes one or the other.
- The factory workers who make Honey Bunches of Oats act like they're personally responsible for the cereal satisfaction of every person on the planet.
- If I use a certain whitening toothpaste, not only will it land me a boyfriend, but I'll also be able to land planes at night due to the brightness of my choppers.

Advertising dollars well spent.

Nothing to Sneeze At

While I generally reserve my judgment of people until they say something stupid, I have to admit that I have an unnatural distrust of people who hold in their sneezes to sound like little dainty mouse squeaks.

There is nothing natural about this, and if they can't be trusted to honor the natural cleansing of one's nasal passages of harmful things like germs and irritants, what else are they hiding?

One can never be sure.

But on some level, I suppose I can relate.

I don't have a cute little button nose. My nose has a bump in the middle and is anything but little and cute.

But the nose I have is the same nose that my grandpa had, my mom has and a majority of my aunts, uncles and cousins have. Along with pierogi, a love of baseball and politically incorrect humor, carrying on this Polish protuberance is sort of like a family seal.

This family seal also produces loud sneezes.

When I was in elementary school I used to dread having a test, mostly because the room would be so quiet that if and when I had to sneeze, I would blow the minds (and possibly eardrums) of my classmates.

I would try everything to prevent it from happening. Holding my breath didn't work. Putting my finger or a tissue/sleeve under my nose didn't work (but did result in having something to catch whatever flew out at the time.) Eventually I just accepted that you can't stop sneezing from happening, just like you can't sneeze with your eyes open.

And I've also accepted that sneezing while driving is quite possibly the scariest thing ever.

At any rate, when somebody sneezes I feel compelled to reactively bless them for expelling harmful things like germs and irritants through their beak — even the weirdoes that hold sneezes in.

And despite the fact I'm not religious, not saying, "Bless you" feels uncomfortable and wrong on some level.* I do it for everyone, even strangers who occasionally look at me like I just told them Richard Simmons was starring in "Rambo."

*However, after two sneezes I will no longer bless you. At that point you have exhausted my well of goodwill and quite frankly, you're on your own.

To me, it's just a polite courtesy, something that let's them know, "Hey there. It's okay to sneeze and not try to hold it back in. Kumbaya, Hakuna Matata and gesundheit."

Here's a tissue.

If You Can't Take the Heat

Despite the fact that my cooking style is not a style at all, I love food shows like "Restaurant: Impossible," "Unwrapped" and those that are competition-related.

I enjoy seeing people running around kitchens and getting judged on things that will never happen in real life — like creating 1,000 cupcakes in two hours or seeing the Iron Chef chairman back-flip into the kitchen with a sword and orders to cook a whole meal with a walnut.

I also realize they're bit ridiculous, so I've included a few things you can expect to see almost every episode from a couple of them that I watch.

Hell's Kitchen

The gist is 18 competitors subject themselves to verbal abuse and backstabbing manipulation in an attempt to cook their way into a head chef position at one of Ramsay's restaurants.

With his reputation on the line, Gordon doesn't take any of the bull crap. This produces a lot of colorful dialogue, gourmet dishes and the illusion that the cooks have learned something other than British profanity.

- When actually asked to cook, contestants suddenly forget how to boil water and Gordon will throw things at them.
- Someone will overcook fish and undercook rice, crimes ranking second only to "being a cow" in the world of Ramsay.
- Gordon will yell, "Shut it down!" in the middle of the service.
- Gordon will yell, "This is raw! You're going to kill somebody!"
- Gordon will yell that every service is "the worst dinner service in history!"
- Contestants will sell out their mother in a dramatic tribal counsel-like elimination ceremony in an effort to not have their picture burned as the show fades to the closing credits.

- When dramatically forced to give over their apron, the eliminated chef will say, "you haven't seen the last of me." You will have seen the last of them.

Moral of the story: It's scripted and over the top, but I take what I can get. Also, don't ever make a mistake or Gordon will throw it at you.

Chopped

Four chefs compete before a panel of three expert judges to create a three-course meal in under 30 minutes or so with "mystery ingredients" found in a basket. Once they're done, they present each course to the unenthused judges and one chef gets chopped. The winner gets $10,000.

- First of all, the secret ingredient in every single dish is sweat. Although entertaining to watch, you'll be completely grossed out and wonder how anyone can eat anything presented.
- Whoever creates the basket is a sadistic bastard. "For the dessert round, you have to use unicorn horn, pancetta, pink currants, crème fraiche." Really?
- At least one contestant will bring up the fact they're self-taught, are competing for a dying relative or that they "didn't come here to lose." *(That's probably a good competition strategy.)*
- One of the judges will flap their hands around in the final seconds of a round yelling, "just get something on the plate!" and then bitch about whatever ended up on the plate.
- The host — Ted Allen — will inevitably try to talk to a contestant while they are moving really fast, get in their way and stress them out even more.
- After forgetting to use a required ingredient or stabbing Ted when he tried to talk to them, a contestant will angrily blame the judges, the oven or the contestants for losing.
- When interviewed, they will say, "you haven't seen the last of me." You will have seen the last of them.

Moral of the story: The only way I could compete on this show is if the basket ingredients were avocado, sprouted grain bread and Bobby Flay himself.

Perishable Puns

It started off simple enough with this lame Facebook status:

"I'm just a fungi with high morels looking to shoot the shiitake with a cute little button like you." -Mushroom at a single's bar.

To put it in a nutshell, people relished the update and even mustard up the strength to ketchup with me and contribute to the fray *(there was mushroom for improvement.)* So that simple update planted the seed for this post, a series of perishable personal ads you probably won't find on Craig's List.

Dig in.

Hi. I'm Herb. I've been hurt before, but I'm gingerly throwing my caraway and trying to find love one more thyme. While I'm no sage, chive got a feeling that if we share some common interests— conversation peppered with laughs, the desire to curry on a new friendship—thistle work and we'll become the pesto friends.

Born and bread in Coloradough, I'm just a simple guy wondering what I am doughing here. My past attempts at dating have gone a-rye, and I've found myself in seedy bars with weirdoughs thinking, "I donut belong here." But I figured I kneaded to try this again, and placing an ad was the yeast I could do. I'm looking for someone to loaf around with who is willing to go against the grain, roll with the punches and rise to any occasion. If this is you, please reply and I will millet over.

Well-cultured woman looking for a gouda time with a minimal margarine for error. It a curd to me that I in no whey deserve to settle for less than jam-packed excitement—which is a nice way of pudding it—so the more spontaneous you are, the butter. I cannoli imagine the fun we will have!

Single chick with chili disposition looking to stop floundering around. Past dating experiences have been offal, dare I say the wurst, and I won't make that missed steak again! I'm accident prawn with a bit of a fowl mouth, but would love to meat someone who I can bacon for companionship and fun. If that sounds like ewe, carpe diem!

I yam hoping this ad will produce some grate replies, as I'm tired of medi-okra dates with men who think a huge celery means we make a great pear. Bean there, done that and sometimes I wonder why I even carrot all. But if you march to the beet of your own drum, lettuce meet and see what might turnip.

I know. I know. Any way you slice it, these are corny and I falafel about how cheesy they are. But don't worry…I won't milk this anymore.

That's a wrap.

Live and Learn

I am no expert on anything other than how *not* to do various activities, but I have still learned a few things in my 31 years. So while I don't always follow my own advice — or remember everything that I say — I'm sharing a few things below:

1. The universe owes you nothing. You owe it to yourself to make things work.
2. You can get through anything if don't look too far past today.
3. Righty tighty, lefty loosey.
4. You don't have to win—or participate in—every argument.
5. It's far more impressive when others discover your good qualities without you having to tell them.
6. There are those who dust and then vacuum and those who vacuum and then dust. The latter group is wrong, by the way.
7. Work is work. Most people don't love their job, but most people also need money.
8. Time spent doing what you like is never time wasted.
9. Hurt people hurt people. Often those who are the hardest to love are the ones who need it the most.
10. The best way to make yourself feel better about having to wait in a long line is to look at the people behind you.
11. Teeth are jewels, not tools.
12. If a relationship has to be a secret, you shouldn't be in it.
13. You learn by doing, even—*or especially*—if that means doing something wrong.
14. For every action, there is an equal and opposite overreaction.
15. There is no baseline for normal. Once you realize this, it takes the pressure off.
16. What you do every day is more important than what you do once in a while.
17. Share.
18. Make peace with your past so it won't screw up the present.
19. Non-stick pans and self-cleaning ovens? Lies, nothing but lies.
20. Everyone has a story. Not everyone has plans and not excuses.
21. A writer writes. A painter paints. Action trumps intention.
22. The best sign of a healthy relationship is that there's no sign of it on Facebook.

23. People think their way out of doing everything that's worth doing in life.
24. Read. Books.
25. Sometimes life does give you more than you can handle. Never be ashamed to ask for help.
26. Don't pull the tail of a goat or scratch the top of a buffalo's head.
27. Envy is a waste of time. Be better, not bitter.
28. If you have more than one junk drawer, you have too much junk.
29. Take your time.
30. Everything can change in the blink of an eye.
31. If a car is held together with masking tape and plastic wrap, always let them merge. They obviously have nothing to lose.
32. Drop the ego. Don't take yourself so seriously. No one else does.
33. No. 32 is really hard.
34. Busyness does not equate with productivity.
35. However good or bad a situation is, it will change.
36. People rarely RSVP to pity parties.
37. Thinking, "Could I make a bigger mess?" is basically just issuing a challenge to yourself.
38. No matter how lonely you might feel, there is *always* someone who can relate to you.
39. Never judge a book by its movie.
40. If you mean it, say "I love you." Say it often.
41. You can—and will—always be humbled by something or someone. This is a good thing.
42. Overprepare and then go with the flow.
43. When in doubt, just take the next small step—even if you're clumsy.
44. Old people are wise beyond our years.
45. Sundays are for washing floors and clothes, not for washing hair.
46. If you don't ask, you don't get.
47. "Believe nothing, no matter where you read it or who has said it, unless it agrees with your own reason and your own common sense." –Buddha
48. I hate ending things on an odd number, so this is the last one is basically filler.

Liquor Before Beer, Never Fear

There are a lot of people who like beer.

In fact, a majority of people I know love beer and I'm pretty sure I could have paid for my college tuition with bottle returns from family functions if my crazy uncle didn't hoard them every time so he could buy batteries for his metal detector.

But I, for one, couldn't care less about beer. In fact, I've never had more than a sip of the stuff and despite the fact that it would be a cheaper option than my Vodka for the couple times a year I have a drink, I have no desire to try and acquire a taste for it.

Is it because I worked as a cocktail waitress the summer of my 21st birthday and the exposure to dollar drafts and douchebags debauchery turned me off?

Possibly, but that didn't stop me from "sowing my oats" and celebrating that whole summer. I have stories, but I also have memories of having to serve Mexican food while nursing the worst hangover of my life due to an ill-advised Four Horseman shot and half a bottle of Vanilla Stoli after work the night/early morning before at a frat house.

It's been more than a decade and I still can't smell vanilla without getting nauseous.

At any rate, I never took to beer. I also tried to like wine, but it gave me a headache and reminded me of church, which just made me feel guilty on top of feeling hung-over.

But that brings me to the stereotypical beer vs. wine person debate.

There used to be this image of beer drinkers being "everyday" blue collar workers asking for Busch in a can at a restaurant and crushing the can on their foreheads, while wine drinkers were women who "did lunch" and requested pinot with their pedicures.

When I was serving I had a woman who always sat on the patio and ordered draft beer in a wine glass because she wanted to drink beer but look classy to the people walking by.

Yes, because fine wine always has a tan hue and a head of foam.

Anyway, at least around my city, microbreweries and beer festivals have been popping up just as much as wine bars and vineyard tours. It's not just Miller Lite now, but beer with ingredients like fruit, chocolate and coffee, meaning there are more options and more people taking to the hops.

This also means the stereotypical "lines" are blurred and there are now beer snobs and wine pounders, wine snobs and beer pounders, men who drink wine, women who drink beer and that weirdo who will ask for her beer in a wine glass.

I still get confused with all the options and considering the fact that I've only tried the crap from the tap and not some hoity-toity mix of hops, I admit I can't really say I don't like beer.

However, I don't think I'm willing to try.

If I'm feeling the need to imbibe, I'll just spend my money on a Vodka gimlet, fully aware that one is all it takes to turn this lightweight into an (even more) unfiltered karaoke queen ready to perform "Baby Got Back" with the enthusiasm of a used car salesman doing his own commercials.

Who are we kidding?

I still do that sober.

Avoid Clichés like the Plague

There is no shortage of inspirational quotes or tired clichés on the Internet, and I have to admit that I'm guilty of occasionally using them myself.

But most of the time I'm much more Abby-like, putting my own spin on conventional wisdom and taking the lion's share of the credit *(see what I did there? Picking up what I'm putting down?)*

So sit back, relax and, you know, take what I say with a grain of salt.

Another day, another dollar that won't be accepted in the self-checkout lane register despite the fact that only one tiny little corner of the bill is slightly wrinkled.

An apple a day keeps the doctor away, but if you throw it hard enough, it can pretty much repel anyone in any profession.

Dance like nobody is watching, unless you're in the grocery store and "Footloose" comes on. At that point, performing the role of Ren is generally frowned upon *(although they are only encouraging this behavior by playing that song in the store.)*

Be the change you want to see in the world. By that I mean change the freaking roll of toilet paper or paper towel when there's only one sheet left, you heathen.

Birds of a feather flock together and usually decide to use my Blazer as their own personal overpriced outhouse.

Misery loves company, which is why I prefer to stay away from people when possible.

Sometimes you're the windshield. Sometimes you're the bug. Most often you're the driver behind the windshield trying like hell to pump the windshield wipers and clean off the splattered bug guts.

Do not go where the path may lead, go instead where there is no path and wear huge shoes so people think they're tracking the Bigfoot.

A watched pot never boils, but if you turn your back for five seconds it will boil over and make a mess of your stove.

Good fences make good neighbors, as they don't judge when I do my Saturday morning walk of shame to the trash can in my pajamas to throw away the cat litter or chase off the freaking woodchuck.

Never put off until tomorrow what you can do today, unless it's something unpleasant that someone else might just do before you. In that case, carry on.

Slow and steady wins the race—except races in which the point is to finish first, which is basically most races.

Do one thing every day that scares you, unless that involves going to Wal-Mart on a Saturday afternoon and possibly being sexually harassed by exposed ass cracks and muffin tops. *(Pick a different challenge that day.)*

It is never too late to be what you might have been, unless your goal was to be a child prodigy or unicorn, in which case you're basically screwed.

We are what we repeatedly do. Excellence, then, is not an act, but a habit. That also means your bitchiness isn't a mood, but rather your personality.

Do as I say, not as I — hell, you should probably just do what I say and be done with it. Better safe than sorry.

Hyperthetically Speaking

When people hear I'm an editor, the first thing they often assume is that I'm the grammar police. I am not.

While I unfortunately/reflexively think in AP Style and know the difference between "that" and "which," that doesn't mean I'm not constantly referring to the AP Stylebook at work or that I always remember that a preposition is something never to end a sentence with.

And I've accepted—*not excepted*—the fact that I will never be able to correctly spell words like definitely on my first or third try. But there are a few things that do make me lose—*not loose*—my cool with how language is often used.

Aha! There is one of them!

Lately the word "used" is being replaced by "utilize"—one of those "smart" words people throw into in hoping to sound fancy or amazingly intelligent.

Quick lesson: The definition of *utilize* implies taking something and using it for an unintended purpose (*convert to use.*) Meanwhile, the definition of *use* means employing any old thing to achieve your goal, whether or not you use that any old thing for its intended purpose. So if you are not actually creating an alternate use for something, *utilize* is the wrong word.

Don't use it.

With that out of the way, I have to admit that I do have a list of other words that I have personally witnessed the abuse of on multiple occasions, and I don't feel bad specifically—*not pacifically*—pointing out these examples.

It's not me being especially—*not expecially*—picky, but rather being helpful. Because I can tell you from a professional standpoint that for all intents and purposes—*not intensive purposes*—if you say/type something incorrectly, there's a chance that someone could have — *not could of* — misunderstood what you were trying to say.

So occasionally pointing out to someone that "spelt" is a type of wheat and "spelled" is what they've done incorrectly is actually a public service.

Regardless — *not irregardless, mind you* — I figured I could probably — *not prolly* — vent my frustrations — *not flusterations* — here of a couple things I have seen *(not saw.)*

Hypothetically — *not hyperthetically* — speaking, let's say you are engaging in an email conversation with someone and they asked — *not axed* — you if you had talked to a certain individual about his work ethic — *not work ethnic.*

A reply of, "He surposedly/supposably logged in five hours on Monday" will appear confusing to the recipient because "surposedly" is not a real word and "supposably," although a real word that means "able to be supposed," is not a synonym for "supposedly."

I could go on with another — *not nother* — example or two, but that would probably just sound too petty. In general, I really couldn't care less about a lot of these except the misuse of "could care less" vs. "couldn't care less." That one just pisses me off.

Plus, I know that sometimes it's simply a matter of hitting the wrong key on the keyboard, like the time I shared that I was "super busty" instead of "super busy." *(Looks up at the sky, twiddling her thumbs and innocently whistling a tune.)*

After all, mistakes happen — hypothetically speaking, of course.

Letters I Probably Won't Send

To the Man in front of me at the Dollar Store buying a fake rose, lip balm, K-Y Jelly and three servings of potted meat:

I'm not sure if I should be disgusted at this unique combination of purchases or admire you for your effort and optimism. The fake rose is admirable, but if you are in fact planning for a romantic evening with someone other than yourself— as your purchase of K-Y Jelly instead of lotion and Kleenex would suggest — the addition of potted meat is quite troubling.

Putting aside the fact I only eat plants and would rather eat the metal pot than the "meat" your potted meat contains, the Dollar Store does offer a variety of other edible creations that might help to set a more "romantic" mood—canned oysters *(aphrodisiac!)* crackers or even a cupcake mix *(chocolate!)* might be a better solution.

And K-Y Jelly from the Dollar Store? Remember that you get what you pay for, and take note of the woman behind me the other day who filled her cart with at-home pregnancy tests, ovulation kits and Cheetos. Prevention is key, my friend.

To the Man at the Dollar Store who kept asking his wife how much something costs:

It's $1. Everything is $1. Beware, as your wife looks annoyed and might just throw a dull off-brand pair of kitchen shears into the cart. Sleep with one eye open.

And to your wife? Take a deep breath and count to 10. Thousand.

To commercials targeted at women:

While I understand the marketing idea behind making everyday situations appear a million times more exciting than they actually are, most of us are not fooled into thinking that using a whitening toothpaste will in fact make our teeth so white that our smile could land a husband or a small aircraft or that wiping up spills with extra-absorbent paper towel makes us want to sing.

I also don't invite friends over to watch me dance with a miracle mop and then eat the yogurt you pimp out that the reaction of women in commercials would have me believe contains orgasmic properties and not just probiotics.

As for expressing my individuality, I don't need to do it through pink pens or feminine hygiene products packaged in bright colors with cool patterns, but thank you for the suggestion.

To the sock that falls out of the laundry basket as I'm walking up the stairs:

You might not think this is a big deal and that you deserve some "alone" time away from the crowd, but you have to understand the implications of your escape.

As I bend down to pick you up — basket full of laundry in my arms — it's inevitable that at least two other items from the basket will also jump ship. I also have to pick up a towel and/or a dishcloth that has fallen while I'm down there to pick you up and the cycle just goes on and on.

You can see how distressing this is, and quite honestly, your behavior gives me reason to believe that *you* are why the divorce rate of my socks is increasing. Let's work on this, little buddy.

To the cashier who said, "Enjoy your evening!" as I left the store carrying my box of Q-tips and a bottle of oven cleaner:

I think it goes without saying that I'll do just that.

It's the Little Things

We've all had those days when nothing monumentally bad happens, but yet there are a bunch of little things that simply make you want to absolutely lose your shit, so to speak.

Big picture? They're not a big deal.

Small picture in that moment? The straw that broke the camel's back. The last thing you need. THE BIGGEST DEAL EVER!

Let's begin, perhaps with someone overusing CAPITAL LETTERS and exclamation points!!!

Anyway, I love my hooded sweatshirts. When it's freezing outside and I want to pretend I'm a turtle with the option to retract myself back into my shell, the hood serves as my delusional means of escape. Plus, it's warm.

But there are times when the string of my hoodie will mysteriously disappear into the depths of the hood itself. Sound the alarm! Call in the rescue squad! This is a traumatic turn of events, as it will then require me to somehow try and manipulate the string back to the opening through the use of tweezers and profanity.

By the time I prove myself as a hoodie hero and restore balance to my universe through the miraculous string rescue, I'm exhausted and ready to retreat back into the comfort of my cotton cocoon. I think I should start a support group.

Let's journey down to the other end of the clothing spectrum and socks.

If you've ever worn snow boots outside, you know the scenario. You come in, try and slip your boots off and move on with your life and find that your sock has been swallowed up into the depths of the boot.

Of course you discover this when you pull out your foot and step down into the pile of snow that your boot has just left on the floor.

The only thing that makes this situation worse is when you go to put your sock back on and discover you have a jagged little piece of toenail that gets stuck on a string inside of the sock, creating a painful, snag-filled scenario or a new hole in the sock and your sanity.

Sigh…let's move on.

Like most people, I enjoy a hot shower. What I don't enjoy is turning off the water of said shower, discovering that although I've just spent 10 minutes in the direct stream of water I've neglected to rinse out my shampoo and that I also forgot to put a new towel on the rack.

The cat is no help.

Then there's this food situation, and for me, anything that involves food is usually a highly-serious "situation" not to be messed with.

There's nothing more disappointing than cutting into an avocado and discovering that it's a) 50 percent pit or b) bruised beyond belief. This can apply to other fruits and vegetables as well, but it will usually only happen to the one item you were REALLY looking forward to eating at that exact moment.

Put down the sharp kitchen objects and slowly back away from the counter. It's not worth it.

Just take a deep breath and retreat into your hoodie. Big picture, things will work out — except finding that string in your hoodie.

It's the Little Things, Part 2

I wrote about those little things that simply make you want to freak out, so to speak.

But in the interest of appearing balanced in at least one facet of my life, I've decided to take the opposite approach and talk about a couple of those delightful surprises that can perk up your day.

Big picture? They're not a big deal. Small picture in that moment? THE BIGGEST DEAL EVER!

Let's begin.

There have been a couple of times when I've spent almost a whole hour attempting to "shop," aka "buy nothing after destroying many piles of neatly folded shirts and vow to never shop for clothes again."

On the rare occasion that I do find something that a) kind of fits b) I don't hate or c) doesn't qualify me for "What Not to Wear," I usually end up not buying it anyway because I'm cheap and have a bigger budget for paper towel than I do for new clothes. But when I do take the purchasing plunge, there is no greater delight than getting up to the register and finding out that the item rang up on sale.

Well, I wouldn't buy it if it wasn't on sale, but I mean like, clearance sale prices! For me? On this shirt I spent 45 minutes pretending to try on over my clothes? It's like the purchase was deemed acceptable by the universe and for that one brief moment in time, shopping isn't pure hell.

The greatest lie I tell myself is that I don't need to write something down, so when I actually remember the great idea I had either right before I fell asleep or stepped into the shower, it totally makes my day.

Going back to clothes, how great is it to reach into your coat or pants pocket and find something like a $5 bill? I'll tell you — pretty great.

In fact, sometimes when I put away my winter coats for the year, I will stick a small bill in the pocket as a little present for myself when the snow rolls around the next year…or when I remember it's there during the summer and need $5 for the Farmer's Market. Whatever.

What's even better than finding $5 in the pocket of your coat? How about finding one more of whatever kind of food thing you're craving you thought was gone forever — a piece of chocolate found in the cupboard, a container of frozen deliciousness shoved in the back of the freezer, one more piece of Shredded Wheat that fell out of your shirt when you stood up.

If you ask me, that's like winning the lotto.

Because I'm a dinosaur, I do not have an iPod or anything similar to that. For that reason, it's kind of awesome to get into my car and find my favorite song just started, meaning I get to listen to it in it's entirety — singing at the top of my lungs like the car karaoke queen that I am — without driving around the block to hear the end or cursing the fact I missed the beginning.

Knowing people found my blog with "bedazzled squirrel life preservers," "it's chickpeas, not dudepeas" and "Eminem wearing a babushka and shitkicker boots."

Like I said, it's the little things.

Shocking Plot Twists

While I love my routines, I hate predictability when it comes to the storylines in books, TV shows and movies. If I can figure out what's going to happen five minutes in, you've lost me.

So I present to you a more realistic view of some stories you might have been told.

Shocking Plot Twists and Untold Stories, Revealed!

Belle *(Beauty)* and the Beast split up shortly after they realize they don't have any dishes or household products that actually work. If you will recall, theirs spend a majority of the time singing and dancing.

While entertaining at first, it soon became evident that a talking candlestick and chipped, chatty tea cup don't do much more than provide an audience for the newlyweds as they argue about hair in the sink and the fact that Belle's dad won't move out.

With Yogi taking the role of the friendly picnic basket thief, Smokey the Bear was discovered to actually be the one starting a majority of forest fires. In an attempt to maintain job security, Smokey apparently felt his only inroad to fame was deceit and a penchant for arson.

If you give a mouse a cookie, he will not ask for a glass of milk, want to look in a mirror to make sure he doesn't have a milk mustache, etc. like the story would have you believe. Instead he will try and take residence up in the pantry, crap all over and fall victim to an edible eviction at the hands of a domestic feline who can sniff out fear and fur.

As it turns out, the beautiful Rapunzel doesn't let her hair down just for any man—she lets it down for every man. After leading the love-struck fools into her web of hair extensions and thinly-spread lies for too long, friends and family stage an intervention. However, Rapunzel instead decides to cut off her hair, sell it on eBay and try out for "The Bachelor."

CSI Episode: No one is killed. The detectives hang in the office and play Bananagrams.

Philosophical differences between neighbors Johnny Appleseed, a kind soul who loves to plant apple trees and protect them from harm, and Paul Bunyan, a testosterone egomaniac who cuts down the trees with one swoop of his axe, land these two on Judge Judy.

It gets dirty. Johnny brings up how Paul never picks up the literal bull shit that Babe the Blue Ox leaves around. Paul counters with an argument about property lines and the tree that is actually his. Judge Judy sighs, rolls her eyes and rules in favor of Johnny because Paul wore jeans into court. Her ruling is final.

After hearing about Snow White's brush with a necrophilia-driven Prince, an evil Queen and a life filled with cooking, cleaning and keeping house for seven "little people" while they mine for jewels and go out at night, TLC offers Snow White her own reality show.

The only requirement is that she incorporate the dwarfs and cupcakes somehow to appeal to their core demographic. She accepts and "Good Things Come in Small Packages" is a huge hit.

The Little Engine that Could, best known for optimistically chanting, "I think I can, I think I can," could overcome every seemingly impossible task except being cited for EPA clean air violations. He thought he could, but he can't — until he cleans up his act.

We'll end with the first story told — Adam and Eve.

However, in this instance Eve says she can't eat the apple because there's no proof that it's 100 percent non-GMO organic. Adam, annoyed and exasperated with Eve—but more importantly, ravenously hungry — grabs the apple, his junk behind the strategically-placed fig leaf and chows down.

I think we know how this ends.

What I've Learned from Blogging

I've been blogging for a couple years now, and over that time I've come to learn certain things, like I rarely make a long story short and how to make a picture bigger than a thumbnail *(this took two years, people.)*

And while I know it's boring to write about blogging, I thought I would share a few things I've learned *(the first one evidently being I can write about whatever I want to.)*

Why I Write

I write because I have to. It gets me out of my head and makes me feel productive and creative and useful. When I feel I have nothing to say, I get pissy. When I get on a roll, I get almost annoyingly cheerful. I feel emotion, which is rare, and that's how I know it's important to me.

I Can Be Funny

I've learned it's okay to be confident and I think I can be pretty funny. While that will never lead to fame and fortune, I like knowing I make someone laugh or think—even if it's only my mom. Hi, Mom!

People Are Awesome

I can connect with a bazillion awesome people that I would never have met otherwise, and honestly, you people save my life. I never really thought I "needed" people, but I do. And to those who say "online friends" aren't real, I will counter with the fact that if cyber bullying can and does exist, so can cyber connections.

So there.

You Can Click Away

Not everyone will like you and you won't like everyone else. You don't have to tell everyone all your opinions. People will disappoint you. Their blogs will change, they will sell out or maybe you'll just grow apart. Don't take it personally, and don't begrudge them for choosing their path — even if that path is really annoying and lame.

Social Media Can Rock

On one hand, it's awesome because you can connect with the bazillion awesome people I mentioned above. When I promote a post, it's not for validation — it's because I think you might like it and I want to share. And I love my blog's Facebook page and comments because people interact and make me laugh or think. Muah! Big cyber air kiss!

Social Media Can Suck

But on the other hand, holy hell with the requests for retweets and sharing and a constant barrage of *all the things*! It's come to the point where the writing is no longer enough. Now it's about getting read, no matter what is written, and getting tweeted, pinned, Facebooked, etc. by the greatest number of people.

The end some posts read like a totem pole with eight different icons of where you can find the blogger who is so busy writing and building a brand that they don't have time to read your blog but be sure to read theirs, share the post and vote for them in a contest!

No thanks. I don't understand Instagram, Redditt, etc. and YouTube has a video of a turtle eating a raspberry that I'm pretty cool with.

See "click away" point up above.

It's a Hobby

I get that there's a constant blogging popularity contest going on, but when it comes to aggressively pimping myself out, I'll pass.

It would be great to be able to make a living doing something I love, but not at the expense of authenticity or what minimal sanity I have left. I read blogs I enjoy. I don't read blogs I don't enjoy, even if they're "OHMYGOD the most connected blogger ever."

At the end of the day, there are millions of blogs out there and only so many eyes to read them, with even fewer dollars to support them. If you're in it for the money, good luck with that.

I Can Only Be Me

I can be naive. I can be vulnerable. When I can't write I stress out a bit, but only because I want to entertain you. Or more likely because I had to wear a "real" bra for more than five hours, which is probably the reason. Let's be honest.

But long story short, I have issues. So do you.

I've learned that that's more than okay.

ABOUT THE AUTHOR

Abby Heugel is a still a writer and aspiring hermit in Michigan who is waiting to be discovered as either a brilliant blogger, creator of yoga pants that double as lint rollers or professional asparagus eater.

When she wrote the last book, she was also banking on winning the Powerball by now, but obviously that didn't happen. As a result, she's hoping that somebody might buy this book and then send her a winning Powerball ticket and/or contract offering to pay her to blog while being a stay-at-home mom minus the kids.

You can read more of Abby's work at http://abbyhasissues.com/.

Twitter: @abbyhasissues
Facebook: Abby Has Issues